studysync®

Reading & Writing Companion

With Malice Toward None

How can we attain justice for all?

studysync.com

Send all inquiries to:
BookheadEd Learning, LLC
610 Daniel Young Drive
Sonoma, CA 95476

ISBN 978-1-94-973909-1

6 7 8 9 10 11 B&B 26 25 24 23 22
D

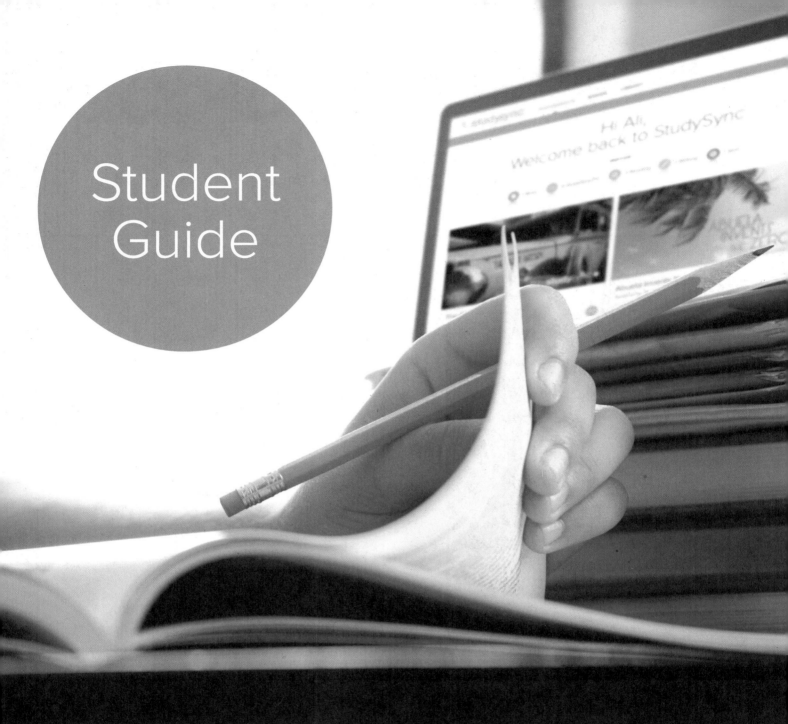

Student Guide

Getting Started

Welcome to the StudySync Reading & Writing Companion! In this book, you will find a collection of readings based on the theme of the unit you are studying. As you work through the readings, you will be asked to answer questions and perform a variety of tasks designed to help you closely analyze and understand each text selection. Read on for an explanation of each

Close Reading and Writing Routine

In each unit, you will read texts that share a common theme, despite their different genres, time periods, and authors. Each reading encourages a closer look through questions and a short writing assignment.

① Introduction

An Introduction to each text provides historical context for your reading as well as information about the author. You will also learn about the genre of the text and the year in which it was written.

② Notes

Many times, while working through the activities after each text, you will be asked to **annotate** or **make annotations** about what you are reading. This means that you should highlight or underline words in the text and use the "Notes" column to make comments or jot down any questions you have. You may also want to note any unfamiliar vocabulary words here.

You will also see sample student annotations to go along with the Skill lesson for that text.

First Read

During your first reading of each selection, you should just try to get a general idea of the content and message of the reading. Don't worry if there are parts you don't understand or words that are unfamiliar to you. You'll have an opportunity later to dive deeper into the text.

Think Questions

These questions will ask you to start thinking critically about the text, asking specific questions about its purpose, and making connections to your prior knowledge and reading experiences. To answer these questions, you should go back to the text and draw upon specific evidence to support your responses. You will also begin to explore some of the more challenging vocabulary words in the selection.

Skills

Each Skill includes two parts: Checklist and Your Turn. In the Checklist, you will learn the process for analyzing the text. The model student annotations in the text provide examples of how you might make your own notes following the instructions in the Checklist. In the Your Turn, you will use those same instructions to practice the skill.

 First Read

Read "The Story of an Hour." After you read, complete the Think Questions below.

THINK QUESTIONS

1. At the beginning of paragraph 9, Mrs. Mallard senses "something coming to her." What is it? What physical effect does it have on her? Cite evidence from the text to support your response.

2. In paragraphs 5 through 9, how do the details about the natural setting outside of Mrs. Mallard's room relate to her emotional state? Point to specific evidence from the text to support your response.

3. At the end of the story, why do the doctors think that Mrs. Mallard died of "the joy that kills"? Do you think their diagnosis is accurate? Cite evidence from the text to support your answer.

4. Use context clues to determine the meaning of the word **elixir**. Then write your best definition of the word here, along with the clues that helped you find it.

5. Use context clues to determine the meaning of the word **absolutely** as it is used in "The Story of an Hour." Write your best definition of *absolutely* here. Then consult a print or online dictionary to confirm its meaning.

 Skill:
Story Elements

Use the Checklist to analyze Story Elements in "The Story of an Hour." Refer to the sample student annotations about Story Elements in the text.

CHECKLIST FOR STORY ELEMENTS

In order to identify the impact of the author's choices regarding how to develop and relate elements of a story or drama, note the following:

- ✓ where and when the story takes place, who the main characters are, and the main conflict, or problem, in the plot
- ✓ the order of the action
- ✓ how the characters are introduced and developed
- ✓ the impact that the author's choice of setting has on the characters and their attempt to solve the problem
- ✓ the point of view the author uses, and how this shapes what readers know about the characters in the story

To analyze the impact of the author's choices regarding how to develop and to relate elements of a story or drama, consider the following questions:

- ✓ How do the author's choices affect the story elements? The development of the plot?
- ✓ How does the setting influence the characters?
- ✓ Which elements of the setting impact the plot, and in particular the problem the characters face and must solve?

YOUR TURN

1. How does Mrs. Mallard's character develop over the course of the short story?
   - ○ A. Mrs. Mallard begins to recognize that prayer is powerful and that she should begin to pray more so that she can live a long life.
   - ○ B. Mrs. Mallard begins to recognize that she is now a free and independent women who has escaped a confined, unhappy life, and this brings her relief, hope, and excitement.
   - ○ C. Mrs. Mallard begins to recognize that she is an independent women, and this scares her and makes her feel very sad and alone.
   - ○ D. Mrs. Mallard transforms from feeling like an uninteresting, boring women to a goddess who will easily be able to find another husband.

2. How does Mrs. Mallard's character development over the course of the short story impact the story's outcome?
   - ○ A. Mrs. Mallard's shift from feeling trapped to feeling free is snatched from her at the very end of the story, causing her death because her new found joy is taken from her.
   - ○ B. Mrs. Mallard shifts from feeling trapped to feeling enraged when she finds out her husband is alive, and her anger causes her death.
   - ○ C. Mrs. Mallard's shift from feeling trapped to feeling free is snatched from her at the very end of the story, and it causes her death because she is overjoyed that her husband is alive.
   - ○ D. Mrs. Mallard shifts from feeling very sad about her husband's death to feeling comforted and relieved that he is alive.

Close Read

6

Reread "The Story of an Hour." As you reread, complete the Skills Focus questions below. Then use your answers and annotations from the questions to help you complete the Write activity.

◎ SKILLS FOCUS

1. Identify details in the beginning of the story that describe how other characters perceive Mrs. Mallard, and explain how this characterization helps develop the plot.

2. Paragraphs 4 through 6 describe aspects of the setting that Mrs. Mallard observes through her window. Highlight the descriptive phrases about the setting that show what Mrs. Mallard sees and explain how these details influence the plot.

3. In paragraphs 9-11, identify textual evidence that shows Mrs. Mallard's reaction to Mr. Mallard's death once she is alone. Then make an inference about how Mrs. Mallard thinks her husband's death will affect her life, and explain how the textual evidence supports that inference.

4. Reread paragraph 14, and use context clues to determine the meaning of the word **impose**. Highlight the clues that help you determine the word's meaning, and annotate with your best definition of the word.

5. What bearing does the idea of independence have on Mrs. Mallard's feelings and actions? How much does she value independence?

✏ WRITE

LITERARY ANALYSIS: How does the author use story elements such as setting, character development, or theme to develop the plot of "The Story of an Hour"? In your response, evaluate at least two of the story elements used by the author and how they shape the plot. Use evidence from the text to support your analysis.

7

At the Foot of the Gallows

FICTION

Introduction

studysync●

8

" At the Foot of the Gallows" tells the story of Ann Hibbins, a Puritan woman who was tried and hanged for witchcraft in Boston in 1656 despite a lack of evidence against her. This work of historical fiction is told from the perspective of a fictional Puritan woman who protests the verdict but is powerless under the same patriarchal, or male-controlled, society that convicted Hibbins.

▽ VOCABULARY

jostle
push against or collide with someone

affrighted
frightened (archaic)

boon
advantage; benefit

indictment
a formal accusation of a crime

8

Close Read & Skills Focus

6

After you have completed the First Read, you will be asked to go back and read the text more closely and critically. Before you begin your Close Read, you should read through the Skills Focus to get an idea of the concepts you will want to focus on during your second reading. You should work through the Skills Focus by making annotations, highlighting important concepts, and writing notes or questions in the "Notes" column. Depending on instructions from your teacher, you may need to respond online or use a separate piece of paper to start expanding on your thoughts and ideas.

Write

7

Your study of each selection will end with a writing assignment. For this assignment, you should use your notes, annotations, personal ideas, and answers to both the Think and Skills Focus questions. Be sure to read the prompt carefully and address each part of it in your writing.

English Language Learner

8

The English Language Learner texts focus on improving language proficiency. You will practice learning strategies and skills in individual and group activities to become better readers, writers, and speakers.

Extended Writing Project and Grammar

This is your opportunity to use genre characteristics and craft to compose meaningful, longer written works exploring the theme of each unit. You will draw information from your readings, research, and own life experiences to complete the assignment.

1 Writing Project

After you have read all of the unit text selections, you will move on to a writing project. Each project will guide you through the process of writing your essay. Student models will provide guidance and help you organize your thoughts. One unit ends with an **Extended Oral Project** which will give you an opportunity to develop your oral language and communication skills.

2 Writing Process Steps

There are four steps in the writing process: Plan, Draft, Revise, and Edit and Publish. During each step, you will form and shape your writing project, and each lesson's peer review will give you the chance to receive feedback from your peers and teacher.

3 Writing Skills

Each Skill lesson focuses on a specific strategy or technique that you will use during your writing project. Each lesson presents a process for applying the skill to your own work and gives you the opportunity to practice it to improve your writing.

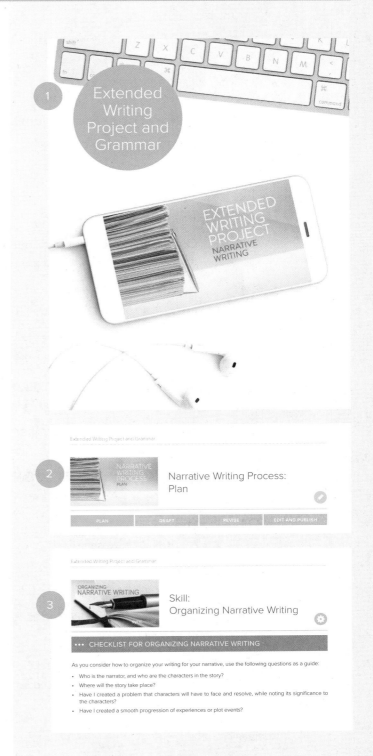

2 Narrative Writing Process: Plan

PLAN · DRAFT · REVISE · EDIT AND PUBLISH

3 Skill: Organizing Narrative Writing

••• CHECKLIST FOR ORGANIZING NARRATIVE WRITING

As you consider how to organize your writing for your narrative, use the following questions as a guide:

• Who is the narrator, and who are the characters in the story?
• Where will the story take place?
• Have I created a problem that characters will have to face and resolve, while noting its significance to the characters?
• Have I created a smooth progression of experiences or plot events?

With Malice Toward None

How can we attain justice for all?

Genre Focus: FICTION

Texts

 Paired Readings

Extended Oral Project and Grammar

English Language Learner Resources

How can we attain justice for all?

CHIMAMANDA NGOZI ADICHIE

Chimamanda Ngozi Adichie (b. 1977) grew up in Nigeria and studied medicine at the University of Nigeria before leaving for the United States to study communications and political science in Philadelphia at Drexel University. She later completed a master's degree from Johns Hopkins University and received a master of arts in African Studies from Yale University. Her novel *Americanah* (2013) was selected as one of "The 10 Best Books of 2013," and won the National Book Critics Circle Award for Fiction. She was awarded a MacArthur Fellowship in 2008.

RITA DOVE

The youngest person and first African American appointed Poet Laureate Consultant by the Library of Congress, Rita Dove (b. 1952) was born in Akron, Ohio. She was a top student and was invited to the White House as a Presidential Scholar. Dove graduated from Miami University in Ohio and received a Fulbright Scholarship, which allowed her to study in Germany. She returned to the United States to earn her master of fine arts from the University of Iowa. Her book *Thomas and Beulah* won the Pulitzer Prize for Poetry in 1987.

RALPH WALDO ELLISON

Ralph Waldo Ellison (1914–1994) is best known for his novel *Invisible Man,* which won the National Book Award. He was born in Oklahoma City, Oklahoma, attended the Tuskegee Institute in Alabama, and then moved to New York City. There, he lived at a YMCA on 135th Street in Harlem and met Langston Hughes and Richard Wright. He was not drafted into World War II, but did enlist in the United States Merchant Marine. Later, he made money writing book reviews but focused on writing Invisible Man. He died of pancreatic cancer at the age of eighty-one.

LOUISE ERDRICH

Louise Erdrich (b. 1954) was born in Little Falls, Minnesota, and attended Dartmouth College, where she was one of the first women admitted to the school. In 1979, she earned a master of arts from Johns Hopkins University. She won numerous awards including the Pushcart Prize in Poetry, the National Book Award for Fiction (*The Round House*), and the Anisfield-Wolf Book Award (*The Plague of Doves*—which was also a finalist for the Pulitzer Prize for Fiction). She currently lives in Minnesota and owns a small independent bookstore.

SKIP HOLLANDSWORTH

At eleven years old, Skip Hollandsworth (b. 1957) and his family moved to Wichita Falls, Texas, where he became interested in the North Texas State Hospital. His fascination with the mental hospital inspired his writing and led him to a career in journalism. In 1979 he graduated with a degree in English from Texas Christian University, where he also served as a sports reporter for the school's paper, the *Daily Skiff.* He has written for the *Dallas Times Herald* and *Texas Monthly*, and his book *The Midnight Assassin* became a *New York Times* bestseller.

MARTIN LUTHER KING JR.

Martin Luther King Jr. (1929–1968) entered college at the age of fifteen and received a BA from Morehouse College. After earning a bachelor of divinity degree and earning his doctorate, he moved to Montgomery, Alabama, in 1954 to become pastor of the Dexter Avenue Baptist Church. Known for his oratorical skills, he led numerous nonviolent protests, including the 1955 bus boycott, the 1963 Birmingham protests, and the March on Washington, where he gave his "I Have a Dream" speech. He was assassinated in Memphis, Tennessee, on April 4, 1968.

ABRAHAM LINCOLN

The 16th president of the United States, the commander in chief of the Union Army during the Civil War, and the first president to be assassinated, Abraham Lincoln (1809–1865) was born in a one-room log cabin on a farm in Kentucky. He served as a captain in the Illinois Militia during the Black Hawk War, as New Salem's postmaster and county surveyor, and was admitted to the Illinois State Bar in 1836. He is best known for preserving the Union, as well as declaring and implementing the legal emancipation of enslaved people in America.

AIMEE NEZHUKUMATATHIL

Born in Chicago, Illinois, Aimee Nezhukumatathil (b. 1974) attended The Ohio State University where she received a bachelor's degree in English, and a master of fine arts in poetry and creative nonfiction. She received the Diane Middlebrook Poetry Fellowship at the Wisconsin Institute for Creative Writing at UW–Madison, and served as the writer-in-residence at the University of Mississippi MFA program from 2016–2017. She is the poetry editor of *Orion magazine,* and her poems have appeared in *Ploughshares, Tin House,* and the *Best American Poetry series.*

TOMÁS RIVERA

Tomás Rivera (1935–1984) was born to migrant farm workers who traveled across Texas and the Midwest following the annual harvest. The first in his family to go to college, Rivera would go on to graduate from Southwest Texas State University where he earned a bachelor's degree in English and a master's degree in education. He received his doctorate from the University of Oklahoma. The author of short stories, poetry, and academic works, Rivera may best be known for the novel *...y no se lo tragó la tierra* (*...And the Earth Did Not Devour Him*).

DALIA ROSENFELD

A graduate of the Iowa Writers' Workshop, a freelance journalist, and creative writing instructor at Bar Ilan University in Israel, Dalia Rosenfeld has appeared in *The Atlantic, Los Angeles Review, Mississippi Review, The Forward,* and the *Michigan Quarterly Review.* She received a Bachelor of Arts in Jewish studies from Oberlin College. Rosenfeld has won the Tobias Wolff Award for Fiction, and the Mississippi Review Prize. She is the author of the short story collection *The Worlds We Think We Know,* and lives in Tel Aviv with her three children.

CHRISTINE KITANO

Christine Kitano was raised in Los Angeles, California, by a first-generation immigrant mother from Korea, and a second-generation Japanese American father. She received her master of fine arts in creative writing from Syracuse University, and her Ph.D. in creative writing from Texas Tech University. She teaches at Ithaca College, where she serves as an assistant professor of creative writing, poetry, and Asian American literature. She is the author of the collections of poetry *Sky Country* and *Birds of Paradise.* She lives in Ithaca, New York.

Postmodernism

Introduction

This introduction provides readers with social and cultural context about the period of history that gave rise to Postmodernism. Confronted with a society increasingly dominated by capitalism and recovering from war, Postmodernist writers were determined to engage in literary experimentation as a way to subvert authority. Learn how Postmodernist writers such as Toni Morrison and Kurt Vonnegut used narrative techniques and genre to challenge their readers' assumptions and societal norms, thereby changing the reading experience altogether.

"A single text can embody a multiplication of meanings."

1 Have you ever read a text and struggled to figure out which character was the protagonist? Have you had difficulty recounting the plot of a film because it was not presented in chronological order? Perhaps in your inability to categorize such a text or film you simply described it as "experimental." It's possible that these representations of dismantled narrative techniques were examples of Postmodernism, a trend that rejects universalities and embraces instability. Postmodernist writing can be difficult to identify because it is the nature of Postmodernism to evade categorization. Much of today's popular media that seem to defy genre characteristics operate within the realm of Postmodernism. Even these texts, however, have patterns and common characteristics. Learning the history of how Postmodernist trends emerged and how they function in contemporary society will better prepare you to see the influence of Postmodernism in your daily life.

Capitalism

2 Postmodernism is not a clear-cut movement with a definitive start and end date. As with other literary trends, many scholars choose to trace the development of Postmodernism in relation to major events in history and their effect on the economy and patterns of cultural expression. For example, comparative literature professor and scholar Fredric Jameson outlines the evolution of realism, Modernism, and Postmodernism according to economist Ernest Mandel's three stages of capitalism:

- The first stage is free-market capitalism, a system in which goods and services are privately owned by individuals or businesses rather than controlled by an authority. In the eighteenth and late nineteenth centuries, Western Europe, England, and the United States witnessed fast-paced technological advancements, such as the growth of the steel industry and steam-driven motors, that made it possible to transport goods and people more efficiently. This period is associated with the development of literary realism and naturalism.

- The next stage of capitalism is monopoly capitalism, a system from the late nineteenth century until the mid-1900s in which corporations became larger and more powerful and international markets were developed. This phase of capitalism is connected to literary Modernism.

- The third stage, **late capitalism** started after World War II and is still happening now. Late capitalism is a post-industrial economic system characterized by globalization, mass media, and consumption. In this modern era of capitalism, the media, consumerism, mass communication, and computer technology are ingrained in everyday life.

3 Many critics agree that the development of Postmodernist thought is concurrent with the emergence of late capitalism. Postmodernists respond to late capitalism with an anti-authoritarian attitude. They reject generalizing theories, universalities, all-encompassing narratives, and ideals constructed by authoritative entities. Early Postmodern writers, such as Kurt Vonnegut, reacted to post-war, post-atomic America in their expressions of antiwar and anti-establishment feelings. Contemporary Postmodern works such as the television series *Black Mirror* often express a distrust in society's reliance on digital networks and surveillance.

Beyond Modernism

4 The Postmodern lens has been applied to such disciplines as philosophy, literature, art, and architecture. The "post" in Postmodern does not identify a time period, but rather a departure from Modernist principles. Modernist texts feature subversive techniques in an effort to demonstrate the inadequacy of outdated literary conventions and to make sense of the chaos in modern life. Modernist writers portray disorder to express their interest in overcoming their disillusionment through the use of new literary forms. Postmodernists engage in similar forms of literary experimentation. For example, **fragmentation**, or the breaking down of narrative conventions, is a common technique in both modern and Postmodern literature. A text might employ fragmentation through non-linear storytelling to disrupt the audiences' reliance on chronology to make sense of events. Or, an author might incorporate an unreliable narrator or multiple narrators to discourage dependency on the experiences of a single character for understanding. However, Modernists and Postmodernists use similar techniques for different purposes. On the one hand, a Modernist might use fragmentation to express a sense of meaninglessness and a desire to ultimately restore order and meaning through new forms. On the other hand, Postmodernists might use fragmentation to underscore the incoherent nature of life and the world. They encourage readers to not only challenge conventions but also to deconstruct literature and to question how meaning is produced.

Hol en Bol by M.C. Escher, 1955. Displayed at the Escher Museum in The Hague, Netherlands.

5 Another key difference between the attitudes of Modernism and Postmodernism is how they conceptualize the roles of the author and the reader. Modernist texts call attention to the author and the control he or she exerts over the text. More emphasis is placed on the inherent subjectivity of a text and how it reflects the interiority of the author or characters. This is exemplified by Modernism's use of interior monologue and stream-of-consciousness narration. Postmodernism is more concerned with how external forces shape what is perceived about a text. Postmodernists often abandon the practice of examining how the author crafted the text to produce a certain meaning and, instead, welcome a new objective purpose in which the meaning of language transforms depending on the perspective of the reader. They generally do not subscribe to the belief that there can be a singular truth or unified means of engagement. As a result, a single text can embody a **multiplication** of meanings.

Major Concepts

Traditions of Non-Tradition

6 Postmodern writers frequently reject overarching interpretations of events that provide a foundation for people's beliefs and give meaning to their experiences. For example, a Postmodernist might respond with skepticism to the claim that anything can be accomplished through hard work and determination. The Postmodernist might seek to point out that such generalizations fail to account for experiences that do not fit within the singular narrative presented.

NOTES

7   In their efforts to dismantle authority, Postmodern narrators often have a self-reflexive voice that draws attention to the text's status as a written work. Self-reflexivity is a characteristic of **metafiction**, or fiction in which the author self-consciously references the fact that the work presented is a literary construction. Examples of Postmodern metafiction include the novel and film *Atonement* which is a story about an author writing a story. The cult classic *The Princess Bride* is a story about a reader reading a story. Lemony Snicket's *A Series of Unfortunate Events* and Roald Dahl's *James and the Giant Peach* both have a narrator who purposefully reveals himself as the author. A metafictional work might also feature a story within a story such as in *The Fault in Our Stars*.

Heterogenous Storytelling

8   Postmodernist literature places an emphasis on a multiplicity of voices and experiences. As such, Postmodernism rejects homogenous storytelling and embraces difference by demanding more visibility for people of color, women, and LGBTQ communities.

9   Some Postmodern authors have engaged with the question of multiplicity of experience with the genre of historiographic metafiction. A term coined by literary theorist Linda Hutcheon, historiographic metafiction is a type of Postmodern literature which combines the techniques of metafiction and historical fiction. According to Hutcheon, such works "are both intensely self-reflexive and yet paradoxically lay claim to historical events." Works of historiographic metafiction, such as Toni Morrison's Pulitzer Prize–winning novel *Beloved,* blend elements of fiction and history to reconsider the past. Historiographic metafiction is just one example of how Postmodern thinking can be used to re-evaluate history and prioritize voices that may have been marginalized in other narratives for a more nuanced view of society.

Adaptation and Amalgamation

10   **Pastiche** is the practice of combining elements of previous works to create something new. This is a common element in Postmodern texts, which tend to imitate the style of, make reference to, or adapt texts from the past. Pastiche can be used to honor the ideas from a previous text or to reinvent them with a unique representation. Stephen Sondheim's musical *Into the Woods* uses pastiche to weave the characters and plots of fairy tales such as "Little Red Riding Hood," "Cinderella," "Rapunzel," and "Jack and the Beanstalk" into one story.

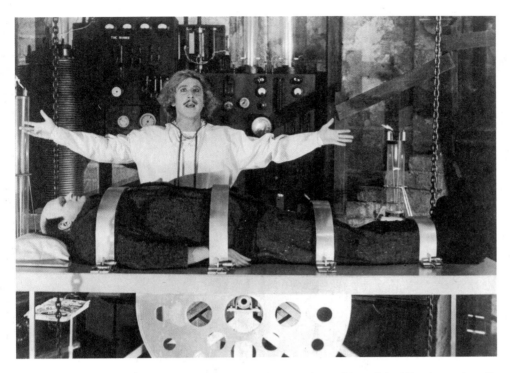

American actor Gene Wilder (1933–2016) stars as the grandson of the original Frankenstein, with Peter Boyle (1935–2006) as the new monster in the Mel Brooks film 'Young Frankenstein', 1974.

11 Postmodern works also make use of **parody**, or work that mimics a style of a work, artist or genre in an exaggerated manner for comedic effect. *Young Frankenstein* (1974), directed by Mel brooks and starring Gene Wilder, adapts Mary Shelley's novel *Frankenstein* in a parody of the horror film genre. The film, shot entirely in black and white, borrows from the style of classic 1930's horror films. Postmodern works can also employ a playful or critical tone through a mixture of highbrow and lowbrow genres that question the value of such distinctions. Highbrow genres are generally considered to be intellectual, sophisticated and serious. Lowbrow genres are regarded as easily accessible and sometimes unrefined. *Young Frankenstein* plays with this hierarchy by repositioning a "classic" text in a new popular culture context. Postmodernists also blend highbrow and lowbrow genres when they play with low and high register vocabularies and grammatical structures; through mixing characteristics and structures of screenwriting, literature, poems, music, ads, news, comics, lists, text messages, etc.; through the use of slang; and by incorporating pop-culture and Americana.

12 Postmodernists encourage audiences to doubt the notion that any text can exist in isolation. They embrace intertextuality, or the references, allusions, and relationships to other texts, to demonstrate how our conceptions of who we are and the world we live in are subject to an endless array of influences.

NOTES

13   Postmodern texts also encourage their audience to take themselves less seriously by denying the existence of set rules or principles and blurring the boundaries between genres.

A piece of graffiti street art, claimed to be by Banksy, shows three stencil figures listening into a conversation in an existing telephone box.

14   **Style and Form**

- Postmodern writing sometimes uses clear, everyday language, though the structure of the text might be very involved. Postmodern writing can include non-traditional or interwoven narratives.

- Popular Postmodernist techniques include an unreliable narrator, ironic narrator, or multiple narrators.

- Postmodernist literature is often easily recognizable through a departure from genre structures, with the incorporation and intermixing of multiple genres.

15   Postmodernism is a far-reaching term that can be applied to a wide range of disciplines. In theory, any text can be read from a Postmodern perspective regardless of whether or not the creator intended it to be ambiguous. Postmodern thinkers interrogate objective proclamations of truth, embracing the echo of interpretation. Where do you draw the line between what is meaningful and what is meaningless? What is purposeful and what is coincidence?

Please note that excerpts and passages in the StudySync® library and this workbook are intended as touchstones to generate interest in an author's work. The excerpts and passages do not substitute for the reading of entire texts, and StudySync® strongly recommends that students seek out and purchase the whole literary or informational work in order to experience it as the author intended. Links to online resellers are available in our digital library. In addition, complete works may be ordered through an authorized reseller by filling out and returning to StudySync® the order form enclosed in this workbook.

Reading & Writing Companion   7

Literary Focus

Read "Literary Focus: Postmodernism." After you read, complete the Think Questions below.

☁ THINK QUESTIONS

1. What is the relationship between late capitalism and Postmodernism? Cite evidence from the text to support your answers.

2. Postmodernists reject overarching concepts about how the world works. How does the use of fragmentation in narratives reflect this purpose? Cite evidence from the text to support your answers.

3. How do Modernists and Postmodernists interpret the roles of the author and the reader differently? Cite evidence from the text to support your answers.

4. The word *multiplication* likely stems from the Latin *multiplico*, meaning "to increase." With this information in mind and using context clues, write your best definition of the word **multiplication** as it used in this text. Cite any words or phrases that were particularly helpful in coming to your conclusion.

5. Use context clues to determine the meaning of the word **pastiche.** Write your best definition here, along with the words and phrases that were most helpful in determining the word's meaning. Then, check a dictionary to confirm your understanding.

Invisible Man

FICTION
Ralph Ellison
1952

Introduction

Winner of the 1953 National Book Award, *Invisible Man* by Ralph Ellison (1914–1994) confronts the social, intellectual, and psychological consequences of living as a black man in America. The unnamed protagonist, who lives rent-free in the forgotten basement of a whites-only apartment on the outskirts of Harlem, tells his life story including his education at Tuskegee, his employment at Liberty Paints in Harlem, and his involvement in a Marxist interracial organization called The Brotherhood. *Invisible Man* is noteworthy not only for its commentary on American race relations but also for its experimental structure, Modernist use of symbolism, stream-of-consciousness narration, and biting satire.

"... and I might even be said to possess a mind."

> Note: Content Advisory: Please be advised that the following text contains graphic descriptions of violence.

From The Prologue

1   I am an invisible man. No, I am not a spook like those who haunted Edgar Allan Poe; nor am I one of your Hollywood-movie **ectoplasms**. I am a man of substance, of flesh and bone, fiber and liquids—and I might even be said to possess a mind. I am invisible, understand, simply because people refuse to see me. Like the bodiless heads you see sometimes in circus sideshows,[1] it is as though I have been surrounded by mirrors of hard, distorting glass. When they approach me they see only my surroundings, themselves, or figments of their imagination—indeed, everything and anything except me.

2   Nor is my invisibility exactly a matter of a bio-chemical accident to my **epidermis**. That invisibility to which I refer occurs because of a peculiar disposition of the eyes of those with whom I come in contact. A matter of the construction of their inner eyes, those eyes with which they look through their physical eyes upon reality. I am not complaining, nor am I protesting either. It is sometimes advantageous to be unseen, although it is most often rather wearing on the nerves. Then too, you're constantly being bumped against by those of poor vision. Or again, you often doubt if you really exist. You wonder whether you aren't simply a phantom in other people's minds. Say, a figure in a nightmare which the sleeper tries with all his strength to destroy. It's when you feel like this that, out of resentment, you begin to bump people back. And, let me confess, you feel that way most of the time. You ache with the need to convince yourself that you do exist in the real world, that you're a part of all the sound and anguish, and you strike out with your fists, you curse and you swear to make them recognize you. And, alas, it's seldom successful.

3   One night I accidentally bumped into a man, and perhaps because of the near darkness he saw me and called me an insulting name. I sprang at him,

---

1. **sideshow** an old-fashioned traveling circus featuring games and sensationalized attractions

seized his coat lapels and demanded that he apologize. He was a tall blond man, and as my face came close to his he looked **insolently** out of his blue eyes and cursed me, his breath hot in my face as he struggled. I pulled his chin down sharp upon the crown of my head, butting him as I had seen the West Indians do, and I felt his flesh tear and the blood gush out, and I yelled, "Apologize! Apologize!" But he continued to curse and struggle, and I butted him again and again until he went down heavily, on his knees, **profusely** bleeding. I kicked him repeatedly, in a frenzy because he still uttered insults though his lips were frothy with blood. Oh yes, I kicked him! And in my outrage I got out my knife and prepared to slit his throat, right there beneath the lamplight in the deserted street, holding him by the collar with one hand, and opening the knife with my teeth—when it occurred to me that the man had not seen me, actually; that he, as far as he knew, was in the midst of a walking nightmare! And I stopped the blade, slicing the air as I pushed him away, letting him fall back to the street. I stared at him hard as the lights of a car stabbed through the darkness. He lay there, moaning on the asphalt; a man almost killed by a phantom. It unnerved me. I was both disgusted and ashamed. I was like a drunken man myself, wavering about on weakened legs. Then I was amused. Something in this man's thick head had sprung out and beaten him within an inch of his life. I began to laugh at this crazy discovery. Would he have awakened at the point of death? Would Death himself have freed him for wakeful living? But I didn't linger. I ran away into the dark, laughing so hard I feared I might rupture myself. The next day I saw his picture in the Daily News, beneath a caption stating that he had been "mugged." Poor fool, poor blind fool, I thought with sincere compassion, mugged by an invisible man!

4   Most of the time (although I do not choose as I once did to deny the violence of my days by ignoring it) I am not so overtly violent. I remember that I am invisible and walk softly so as not to awaken the sleeping ones. Sometimes it is best not to awaken them; there are few things in the world as dangerous as sleepwalkers. I learned in time though that it is possible to carry on a fight against them without their realizing it. For instance, I have been carrying on a fight with Monopolated Light & Power for some time now. I use their service and pay them nothing at all, and they don't know it. Oh, they suspect that power is being drained off, but they don't know where. All they know is that according to the master meter back there in their power station a hell of a lot of free current is disappearing somewhere into the jungle of Harlem. The joke, of course, is that I don't live in Harlem but in a border area. Several years ago (before I discovered the advantage of being invisible) I went through the routine process of buying service and paying their outrageous rates. But no more. I gave up all that, along with my apartment, and my old way of life: That way based upon the **fallacious** assumption that I, like other men, was visible. Now, aware of my invisibility, I live rent-free in a building rented strictly to whites, in a section of the basement that was shut off and forgotten during

Please note that excerpts and passages in the StudySync® library and this workbook are intended as touchstones to generate interest in an author's work. The excerpts and passages do not substitute for the reading of entire texts, and StudySync® strongly recommends that students seek out and purchase the whole literary or informational work in order to experience it as the author intended. Links to online resellers are available in our digital library. In addition, complete works may be ordered through an authorized reseller by filling out and returning to StudySync® the order form enclosed in this workbook.

Reading & Writing Companion   **11**

NOTES

the nineteenth century, which I discovered when I was trying to escape in the night from Ras the Destroyer. But that's getting too far ahead of the story, almost to the end, although the end is in the beginning and lies far ahead.

5 The point now is that I found a home—or a hole in the ground, as you will. Now don't jump to the conclusion that because I call my home a "hole" it is damp and cold like a grave; there are cold holes and warm holes. Mine is a warm hole. And remember, a bear retires to his hole for the winter and lives until spring; then he comes strolling out like the Easter chick breaking from its shell. I say all this to assure you that it is incorrect to assume that, because I'm invisible and live in a hole, I am dead. I am neither dead nor in a state of suspended animation. Call me Jack-the-Bear,[2] for I am in a state of hibernation.

6 My hole is warm and full of light. Yes, full of light. I doubt if there is a brighter spot in all New York than this hole of mine, and I do not exclude Broadway. Or the Empire State Building on a photographer's dream night. But that is taking advantage of you. Those two spots are among the darkest of our whole civilization—pardon me, our whole culture (an important distinction, I've heard)—which might sound like a hoax, or a contradiction, but that (by contradiction, I mean) is how the world moves: Not like an arrow, but a boomerang. (Beware of those who speak of the spiral of history; they are preparing a boomerang. Keep a steel helmet handy.)

7 I know; I have been boomeranged across my head so much that I now can see the darkness of lightness. And I love light. Perhaps you'll think it strange that an invisible man should need light, desire light, love light. But maybe it is exactly because I am invisible. Light confirms my reality, gives birth to my form.

Excerpted from *Invisible Man* by Ralph Ellison, published by Vintage International.

✏️ **WRITE**

DISCUSSION: In small groups, discuss *Invisible Man* as a piece of early Postmodernism. How is your interpretation of Invisible Man influenced by the Postmodern elements Ellison uses, such as fragmentation? To prepare for your discussion, write down at least one element of Postmodernism you have identified in the text.

2. **Jack-the-Bear** a trickster figure from Southern folk stories of anthropomorphized animals

American Horse

FICTION
Louise Erdrich
1991

Introduction

A National Book Award winner, bookstore owner, and member of the Turtle Mountain Band of Chippewa Indians, Louise Erdrich (b. 1954) explores themes of poverty, family, and Native American intercultural dynamics in "American Horse." In this nuanced and empathic work, Erdrich tells the story of Buddy American Horse, a boy torn between the conflicting beliefs of a social worker and the family he loves dearly.

"It doesn't make any difference," she said. "None of it makes any difference."

> Note: Content Advisory: Please be advised that this text contains mature themes, violence, and mildly explicit language.

1   The woman sleeping on the cot in the woodshed was Albertine American Horse. The name was left over from her mother's short marriage. The boy was the son of a man she had loved and let go. Buddy was on the cot too, sitting on the edge because he'd been awake three hours watching out for his mother and besides, she took up the whole cot. Her feet hung over the edge, limp and brown as two trout. Her long arms reached out and slapped at things she saw in her dreams.

Skill:
Story Structure

The story opens with Buddy having a nightmare about hiding from the police. His mother tells him not to worry. He knows something bad is coming. This scene creates immediate tension and seems to foreshadow something bad.

2   Buddy had been knocked awake out of hiding in a washing machine while herds of policemen with dogs searched through the large building with many tiny rooms. When the arm came down, Buddy screamed because it had a blue cuff and sharp silver buttons. "Tss," his mother mumbled, half awake, "wasn't nothing." But Buddy sat up after her breathing went deep again, and he watched.

3   There was something coming and he knew it.

4   It was coming from very far off but he had a picture of it in his mind. It was a large thing made of metal with many barbed hooks, points, and drag chains[1] on it, something like a giant potato peeler that rolled out of the sky, scraping clouds down with it and jabbing or crushing everything that lay in its path on the ground.

5   Buddy watched his mother. If he woke her up, she would know what to do about the thing, but he thought he'd wait until he saw it for sure before he shook her. She was pretty, sleeping, and he liked knowing he could look at her as long and close up as he wanted. He took a strand of her hair and held it in his hands as if it was the rein to a delicate beast. She was strong enough and could pull him along like the horse their name was.

---

1. **drag chains** chains put on a horse to attach to a harrow rake, used to smooth ground after planting

6   Buddy had his mother's and his grandmother's name because his father had been a big mistake.

7   "They're all mistakes, even your father. But *you* are the best thing that ever happened to me."

8   That was what she said when he asked.

9   Even Kadie, the boyfriend crippled from being in a car wreck, was not as good a thing that happened to his mother as Buddy was. "He was a medium-sized mistake," she said. "He's hurt and I shouldn't even say that, but it's the truth." At the moment, Buddy knew that being the best thing in his mother's life, he was also the reason they were hiding from the cops.

10 He wanted to touch the satin roses sewed on her pink T·shirt, but he knew he shouldn't do that even in her sleep. If she woke up and found him touching the roses, she would say, "Quit that, Buddy." Sometimes she told him to stop hugging her like a gorilla. She never said that in the mean voice she used when he oppressed her, but when she said that he loosened up anyway.

11 There were times he felt like hugging her so hard and in such a special way that she would say to him, "Let's get married." There were also times he closed his eyes and wished that she would die, only a few times, but still it haunted him that his wish might come true. He and Uncle Lawrence would be left alone. Buddy wasn't worried, though, about his mother getting married to somebody else. She had said to her friend, Madonna, "All men suck," when she thought Buddy wasn't listening. He made an uncertain sound, and when they heard him they took him in their arms.

12 "Except for you, Buddy," his mother said. "All except for you and maybe Uncle Lawrence, although he's pushing it."

13 "The cops suck the worst, though," Buddy whispered to his mother's sleeping face, "because they're after us." He felt tired again, slumped down, and put his legs beneath the blanket. He closed his eyes and got the feeling that the cot was lifting up beneath him, that it was arching its canvas back and then traveling, traveling very fast and in the wrong direction for when he looked up he saw three of them were advancing to meet the great metal thing with hooks and barbs and all sorts of sharp equipment to catch their bodies and draw their blood. He heard its insides as it rushed toward them, purring softly like a powerful motor and then they were right in its shadow. He pulled the reins as hard as he could and the beast reared, lifting him. His mother clapped her hand across his mouth.

14 "Okay," she said. "Lay low. They're outside and they're gonna hunt."

Skill:
Point of View

Buddy seems to have unconventional emotions toward his mother. Due to this unconventional point of view, it is hard to tell how much Buddy can be trusted in his opinions of her. His opinions may be unreliable.

15 She touched his shoulder and Buddy leaned over with her to look through the cracks in the boards.

16 They were out there all right, Albertine saw them. Two officers and that social worker woman. Vicki Koob. There had been no whistle, no dream, no voice to warn her that they were coming. There was only the crunching sound of cinders in the yard, the engine purring, the dust sifting off their car in a fine light brownish cloud and settling around them.

17 The three people came to a halt in their husk of metal—the car emblazoned with the North Dakota State Highway Patrol emblem which is the glowing profile of the Sioux policeman, Red Tomahawk, the one who killed Sitting Bull. Albertine gave Buddy the blanket and told him that he might have to wrap it around him and hide underneath the cot. "We're gonna wait and see what they do." She took him in her lap and hunched her arms around him. "Don't you worry," she whispered against his ear. "Lawrence knows how to fool them."

18 Buddy didn't want to look at the car and the people. He felt his mother's heart beating beneath his ear so fast it seemed to push the satin roses in and out. He put his face to them carefully and breathed the deep, soft powdery woman smell of her. That smell was also in her little face cream bottles, in her brushes, and around the washbowl after she used it. The satin felt so unbearably smooth against his cheek that he had to press closer. She didn't push him away, like he expected, but hugged him still tighter until he felt as close as he had ever been to back inside her again where she said he came from. Within the smells of her things, her soft skin, and the satin of her roses, he closed his eyes then, and took his breaths softly and quickly with her heart.

19 They were out there, but they didn't dare get out of the car yet because of Lawrence's big, ragged dogs. Three of these dogs had loped up the dirt driveway with the car. They were **rangy**, alert, and bounced up and down on their cushioned paws like wolves. They didn't waste their energy barking, but positioned themselves quietly, one at either car door and the third in front of the bellied-out screen door to Uncle Lawrence's house. It was six in the morning but the wind was up already, blowing dust, ruffling their short moth-eaten coats. The big brown one on Vicki Koob's side had unusual black and white markings, stripes almost, like a hyena and he grinned at her, tongue out and teeth showing.

20 "Shoo!" Miss Koob opened her door with a quick jerk.

21 The brown dog sidestepped the door and jumped before her, tiptoeing. Its dirty white muzzle curled and its eyes crossed suddenly as if it were zeroing its cross-hair sights in on the exact place it would bite her. She ducked back and slammed the door.

22 "It's mean," she told Officer Brackett. He was printing out some type of form. The other officer, Harmony, a slow man, had not yet reacted to the car's halt. He had been sitting quietly in the back seat, but now he rolled down his window and with no change in expression unsnapped his holster and drew his pistol out and pointed it at the dog on his side. The dog smacked down on its belly, wiggled under the car and was out and around the back of the house before Harmony drew his gun back. The other dogs vanished with him. From wherever they had disappeared to they began to yap and howl, and the door to the low shoebox-style house fell open.

23 "Heya, what's going on?"

24 Uncle Lawrence put his head out the door and opened wide the one eye he had in working order. The eye bulged impossibly wider in outrage when he saw the police car. But the eyes of the two officers and Miss Vicki Koob were wide open too because they had never seen Uncle Lawrence in his sleeping get-up or, indeed, witnessed anything like it. For his ribs, which were cracked from a bad fall and still mending, Uncle Lawrence wore a thick white corset laced up the front with a striped sneakers' lace. His glass eye and his set of dentures were still out for the night so his face puckered here and there, around its absences and scars, like a damaged but fierce little cake. Although he had a few gray streaks now, Uncle Lawrence's hair was still thick, and because he wore a special contraption of elastic straps around his head every night, two oiled waves always crested on either side of his middle part. All of this would have been sufficient to astonish, even without the most striking part of his outfit—the smoking jacket. It was made of black satin and hung open around his corset, dragging a tasseled belt. Gold thread dragons struggled up the lapels and blasted their furry red breath around his neck. As Lawrence walked down the steps, he put his arms up in surrender and the gold tassels in the inner seams of his sleeves dropped into view.

25 "My heavens, what a sight." Vicki Koob was impressed.

26 "A character," apologized Officer Harmony.

27 As a tribal police officer who could be counted on to help out the State Patrol, Harmony thought he always had to explain about Indians or get twice as tough to show he did not favor them. He was slow-moving and shy but two jumps ahead of other people all the same, and now, as he watched Uncle Lawrence's splendid approach, he gazed speculatively at the torn and bulging pocket of the smoking jacket. Harmony had been inside Uncle Lawrence's house before and knew that above his draped orange-crate shelf of war medals a blue-black German luger was hung carefully in a net of flat-headed nails and fishing line. Thinking of this deadly exhibition, he got out of the car and shambled toward Lawrence with a dreamy little smile of welcome

Skill:
Point of View

Harmony uses understatement when he describes Uncle Lawrence as "a character." As a fellow Native American, he is trying to apologize for Lawrence's outlandish behavior without blatantly insulting him.

NOTES

on his face. But when he searched Lawrence, he found that the bulging pocket held only the lonesome-looking dentures from Lawrence's empty jaw. They were still dripping denture polish.

28 "I had been cleaning them when you arrived," Uncle Lawrence explained with acid dignity.

29 He took the toothbrush from his other pocket and aimed it like a rifle.

30 "Quit that, you old idiot." Harmony tossed the toothbrush away. "For once you ain't done nothing. We came for your nephew."

31 Lawrence looked at Harmony with a faint air of puzzlement.

32 "Ma Frere, listen," threatened Harmony **amiably**, "those two white people in the car came to get him for the welfare. They got papers on your nephew that give them the right to take him."

33 "Papers?" Uncle Lawrence puffed out his deeply pitted cheeks. "Let me see them papers."

34 The two of them walked over to Vicki's side of the car and she pulled a copy of the court order from her purse. Lawrence put his teeth back in and adjusted them with busy workings of his jaw.

35 "Just a minute," he reached into his breast pocket as he bent close to Miss Vicki Koob. "I can't read these without I have in my eye." He took the eye from his breast pocket delicately, and as he popped it into his face the social worker's mouth fell open in a **consternated** O.

36 "What is this," she cried in a little voice.

37 Uncle Lawrence looked at her mildly. The white glass of the eye was cold as lard. The black iris was strangely charged and menacing.

38 "He's nuts," Brackett huffed along the side of Vicki's neck. "Never mind him."

39 Vicki's hair had sweated down her nape in tiny corkscrews and some of the hairs were so long and dangly now that they disappeared into the zippered back of her dress. Brackett noticed this as he spoke into her ear. His face grew red and the backs of his hands prickled. He slid under the steering wheel and got out of the car. He walked around the hood to stand with Leo Harmony.

40   "We could take you in too," said Brackett roughly. Lawrence eyed the officers in what was taken as defiance. "If you don't cooperate, we'll get out the handcuffs," they warned.

41   One of Lawrence's arms was stiff and would not move until he'd rubbed it with witch hazel in the morning. His other arm worked fine though, and he stuck it out in front of Brackett.

42   "Get them handcuffs," he urged them. "Put me in a welfare home." Brackett snapped one side of the handcuffs on Lawrence's good arm and the other to the handle of the police car.

43   "That's to hold you," he said. "We're wasting our time. Harmony, you search that little shed over by the tall grass and Miss Koob and myself will search the house."

44   "My rights is violated!" Lawrence shrieked suddenly. They ignored him. He tugged at the handcuff and thought of the good heavy file he kept in his tool box and the German luger oiled and ready but never loaded, because of Buddy, over his shelf. He should have used it on these bad ones, even Harmony in his big-time white man job. He wouldn't last long in that job anyway before somebody gave him what for.

45   "It's a damn scheme," said Uncle Lawrence, rattling his chains against the car. He looked over at the shed and thought maybe Albertine and Buddy had sneaked away before the car pulled into the yard. But he sagged, seeing Albertine move like a shadow within the boards. "Oh, it's all a damn scheme" he muttered again.

46   "I want to find that boy and salvage him," Vicki Koob explained to Officer Brackett as they walked into the house. "Look at his family life—the old man crazy as a bedbug, the mother intoxicated somewhere."

47   Brackett nodded, energetic, eager. He was a short hopeful redhead who failed consistently to win the hearts of women. Vicki Koob intrigued him. Now, as he watched, she pulled a tiny pen out of an ornamental clip on her blouse. It was attached to a retractable line that would suck the pen back, like a child eating one strand of spaghetti. Something about the pen on its line excited Brackett to the point of discomfort. His hand shook as he opened the screen door and stepped in, beckoning Miss Koob to follow.

48   They could see the house was empty at first glance. It was only one rectangular room with whitewashed walls and a little gas stove in the middle. They had already come through the cooking lean-to with the other stove and washstand and rusty old refrigerator. That refrigerator had nothing in it but some wrinkled

Please note that excerpts and passages in the StudySync® library and this workbook are intended as touchstones to generate interest in an author's work. The excerpts and passages do not substitute for the reading of entire texts, and StudySync® strongly recommends that students seek out and purchase the whole literary or informational work in order to experience it as the author intended. Links to online resellers are available in our digital library. In addition, complete works may be ordered through an authorized reseller by filling out and returning to StudySync® the order form enclosed in this workbook.

Reading & Writing Companion   19

potatoes and a package of turkey necks. Vicki Koob noted that in her perfect-bound notebook. The beds along the walls of the big room were covered with quilts that Albertine's mother, Sophie, had made from bits of old wool coats and pants that the Sisters sold in bundles at the mission. There was no one hiding beneath the beds. No one was under the little aluminum dinette table covered with a green oilcloth, or the soft brown wood chairs tucked up to it. One wall of the big room was filled with neatly stacked crates of things—old tools and springs and small half-dismantled appliances. Five or six television sets were stacked against the walls. Their control panels spewed colored wires and at least one was cracked all the way across. Only the topmost set, with coathanger antenna angled sensitively to catch the bounding signals around Little Shell, looked like it could possibly work.

49   Not one thing escaped Vicki Koob's trained and cataloguing gaze. She made note of the cupboard that held only commodity flour and coffee. The unsanitary tin oil drum beneath the kitchen window, full of empty surplus pork cans and beer bottles, caught her eye as did Uncle Lawrence's physical and mental deteriorations. She quickly described these "benchmarks of alcoholic dependency within the extended family of Woodrow (Buddy) American Horse" as she walked around the room with the little notebook open, pushed against her belly to steady it. Although Vicki had been there before, Albertine's presence had always made it difficult for her to take notes.

50   "Twice the maximum allowable space between door and threshold," she wrote now. "Probably no insulation. Two three-inch cracks in walls inadequately sealed with whitewashed mud." She made a mental note but could see no point in describing Lawrence's stuffed reclining chair that only reclined, the shadeless lamp with its plastic orchid in the bubble glass base, or the three-dimensional picture of Jesus that Lawrence had once demonstrated to her. When plugged in, lights rolled behind the water the Lord stood on so that he seemed to be strolling although he never actually went forward, of course, but only pushed the glowing waves behind him forever like a poor tame rat in a treadmill.

51   Brackett cleared his throat with a nervous rasp and touched Vicki's shoulder.

52   "What are you writing?"

53   She moved away and continued to scribble as if thoroughly absorbed in her work. "Officer Brackett displays an undue amount of interest in my person," she wrote. "Perhaps?"

54   He snatched playfully at the book, but she hugged it to her chest and moved off smiling. More curls had fallen, wetted to the base of her neck. Looking out the window, she sighed long and loud. "All night on brush rollers for this. What

a joke." Brackett shoved his hands in his pockets. His mouth opened slightly, then shut with a small throttled cluck.

55 When Albertine saw Harmony ambling across the yard with his big brown thumbs in his belt, his placid smile, and his tiny black eyes moving back and forth, she put Buddy under the cot. Harmony stopped at the shed and stood quietly. He spread his arms to show her he hadn't drawn his big police gun.

56 "Ma Cousin," he said in the Michif dialect[2] that people used if they were relatives or sometimes if they needed gas or a couple of dollars, "why don't you come out here and stop this foolishness?"

57 "I ain't your cousin," Albertine said. Anger boiled up in her suddenly. "I ain't related to no pigs."

58 She bit her lip and watched him through the cracks, circling, a big tan punching dummy with his boots full of sand so he never stayed down once he fell. He was empty inside, all stale air. But he knew how to get to her so much better than a white cop could. And now he was circling because he wasn't sure she didn't have a weapon, maybe a knife or the German luger that was the only thing that her father, Albert American Horse, had left his wife and daughter besides his name. Harmony knew that Albertine was a tall strong woman who took two big men to subdue when she didn't want to go in the drunk tank. She had hard hips, broad shoulders, and stood tall like her Sioux father, the American Horse who was killed threshing in Belle Prairie.

59 "I feel bad to have to do this," Harmony said to Albertine. "But for godsakes, let's nobody get hurt. Come on out with the boy, why don't you? I know you got him in there."

60 Albertine did not give herself away this time. She let him wonder. Slowly and quietly she pulled her belt through its loops and wrapped it around and around her hand until only the big oval buckle with turquoise chunks shaped into a butterfly stuck out over her knuckles. Harmony was talking but she wasn't listening to what he said. She was listening to the pitch of his voice, the tone of it that would tighten or tremble at a certain moment when he decided to rush the shed. He kept talking slowly and reasonably, flexing the dialect from time to time, even mentioning her father.

61 "He was a damn good man. I don't care what they say, Albertine, I knew him."

----

2. **Michif dialect** also known as French Cree, spoken generally by older descendents of indigenous people and European fur trappers on the central plains of Canada and in the upper central continental United States

NOTES

62　Albertine looked at the stone butterfly that spread its wings across her fist. The wings looked light and cool, not heavy. It almost looked like it was ready to fly. Harmony wanted to get to Albertine through her father but she would not think about American Horse. She concentrated on the sky blue stone.

63　Yet the shape of the stone, the color, betrayed her.

64　She saw her father suddenly, bending at the grille of their old gray car. She was small then. The memory came from so long ago it seemed like a dream— narrowly focused, snapshot-clear. He was bending by the grille in the sun. It was hot summer. Wings of sweat, dark blue, spread across the back of his work shirt. He always wore soft blue shirts, the color of shade cloudier than this stone. His stiff hair had grown out of its short haircut and flopped over his forehead. When he stood up and turned away from the car, Albertine saw that he had a butterfly.

65　"It's dead," he told her. "Broke its wings and died on the grille." She must have been five, maybe six, wearing one of the boy's tee-shirts Mama bleached in hilex-water.[3] American Horse took the butterfly, a black and yellow one, and rubbed it on Albertine's collarbone and chest and arms until the color and the powder of it were blended into her skin.

66　"For grace," he said.

67　And Albertine had felt a strange lightening in her arms, in her chest, when he did this and said, "For grace." The way he said it, grace meant everything the butterfly was. The sharp delicate wings. The way it floated over grass. The way its wings seemed to breathe fanning in the sun. The wisdom of the way it blended into the flowers or changed into a leaf. In herself she felt the same kind of possibilities and closed her eyes almost in shock or pain, she felt so light and powerful at that moment.

68　Then her father had caught her and thrown her high into the air. She could not remember landing in his arms or landing at all. She only remembered the sun filling her eyes and the world tipping crazily behind her, out of sight.

69　"He was a damn good man," Harmony said again.

70　Albertine heard his starched uniform gathering before his boots hit the ground. Once, twice, three times. It took him four solid jumps to get right where she wanted him. She kicked the plank door open when he reached for the handle and the corner caught him on the jaw. He faltered, and Albertine hit him flat on the chin with the butterfly. She hit him so hard the shock of it

---

3. **hilex-water** referring to Hilex, a brand of bleach

went up her arm like a string pulled taut. Her fist opened, numb, and she let the belt unloop before she closed her hand on the tip end of it and sent the stone butterfly swooping out in a wide circle around her as if it was on the end of a leash. Harmony reeled backward as she walked toward him swinging the belt. She expected him to fall but he just stumbled. And then he took the gun from his hip.

71 Albertine let the belt go limp. She and Harmony stood within feet of each other, breathing. Each heard the human sound of air going in and out of the other person's lungs. Each read the face of the other as if **deciphering** letters carved into softly eroding veins of stone. Albertine saw the pattern of tiny arteries that age, drink, and hard living had blown to the surface of the man's face. She saw the spoked wheels of his iris and the arteries like tangled threads that sewed him up. She saw the living net of springs and tissue that held him together, and trapped him. She saw the random, intimate plan of his person. She took a quick shallow breath and her face went strange and tight. She saw the black veins in the wings of the butterfly, roads burnt into a map, and then she was located somewhere in the net of veins and **sinew** that was the tragic complexity of the world so she did not see Officer Brackett and Vicki Koob rushing toward her, but felt them instead like flies caught in the same web, rocking it.

72 "Albertine!" Vicki Koob had stopped in the grass. Her voice was shrill and tight. "It's better this way, Albertine. We're going to help you." Albertine straightened, threw her shoulders back. Her father's hand was on her chest and shoulders lightening her wonderfully. Then on wings of her father's hands, on dead butterfly wings, Albertine lifted into the air and flew toward the others. The light powerful feeling swept her up the way she had floated higher, seeing the grass below. It was her father throwing her up into the air and out of danger. Her arms opened for bullets but no bullets came. Harmony did not shoot. Instead, he raised his fist and brought it down hard on her head.

73 Albertine did not fall immediately, but stood in his arms a moment. Perhaps she gazed still farther back behind the covering of his face. Perhaps she was completely stunned and did not think as she sagged and fell. Her face rolled forward and hair covered her features, so it was impossible for Harmony to see with just what particular expression she gazed into the head-splitting wheel of light, or blackness, that overcame her.

74 Harmony turned the vehicle onto the gravel road that led back to town. He had convinced the other two that Albertine was more trouble than she was worth, and so they left her behind, and Lawrence too. He stood swearing in his cinder driveway as the car rolled out of sight. Buddy sat between the social worker and Officer Brackett. Vicki tried to hold Buddy fast and keep her arm down at the same time, for the words she'd screamed at Albertine had

Please note that excerpts and passages in the StudySync® library and this workbook are intended as touchstones to generate interest in an author's work. The excerpts and passages do not substitute for the reading of entire texts, and StudySync® strongly recommends that students seek out and purchase the whole literary or informational work in order to experience it as the author intended. Links to online resellers are available in our digital library. In addition, complete works may be ordered through an authorized reseller by filling out and returning to StudySync® the order form enclosed in this workbook.

Reading & Writing Companion   23

NOTES

broken the seal of antiperspirant beneath her arms. She was sweating now as though she'd stored up an ocean inside of her. Sweat rolled down her back in a shallow river and pooled at her waist and between her breasts. A thin sheen of water came out on her forearms, her face. Vicki gave an irritated moan but Brackett seemed not to take notice, or take offense at least. Air-conditioned breezes were sweeping over the seat anyway, and very soon they would be comfortable. She smiled at Brackett over Buddy's head. The man grinned back. Buddy stirred. Vicki remembered the emergency chocolate bar she kept in her purse, fished it out, and offered it to Buddy. He did not react, so she closed his fingers over the package and peeled the paper off one end.

75   The car accelerated. Buddy felt the road and wheels pummeling each other and the rush of the heavy motor purring in high gear. Buddy knew that what he'd seen in his mind that morning, the thing coming out of the sky with barbs and chains, had hooked him. Somehow he was caught and held in the sour tin smell of the pale woman's armpit. Somehow he was pinned between their pounds of breathless flesh. He looked at the chocolate in his hand. He was squeezing the bar so hard that a thin brown trickle had melted down his arm. Automatically he put the bar in his mouth.

76   As he bit down he saw his mother very clearly, just as she had been when she carried him from the shed. She was stretched flat on the ground, on her stomach, and her arms were curled around her head as if in sleep. One leg was drawn up and it looked for all the world like she was running full tilt into the ground, as though she had been trying to pass into the earth, to bury herself, but at the last moment something had stopped her.

77   There was no blood on Albertine, but Buddy tasted blood now at the sight of her, for he bit down hard and cut his own lip. He ate the chocolate, every bit of it, tasting his mother's blood. And when he had the chocolate down inside him and all licked off his hands, he opened his mouth to say thank you to the woman, as his mother had taught him. But instead of thank you coming out he was astonished to hear a great rattling scream, and then another, rip out of him like pieces of his own body and whirl onto the sharp things all around him.

First Read

Read "American Horse." After you read, complete the Think Questions below.

☁ THINK QUESTIONS

1. What do we learn about Vicki Koob from the details she notices about Lawrence's home? Explain, supporting your answer with evidence from the text.

2. What does the memory of the butterfly in the grille add to the arc of the story? Cite evidence from the text to support your response.

3. At the end of the story, what attitude does Buddy have toward Vicki Koob? Provide evidence from the text to support your response.

4. The Latin word *consternare* means "to terrify." Keeping this in mind and using context from the story, what do you think the word **consternated** means? Write your best answer here.

5. What is the meaning of the word **sinew** as it is used in the text? Write your best definition here, along with a brief explanation of how you arrived at its meaning.

Please note that excerpts and passages in the StudySync® library and this workbook are intended as touchstones to generate interest in an author's work. The excerpts and passages do not substitute for the reading of entire texts, and StudySync® strongly recommends that students seek out and purchase the whole literary or informational work in order to experience it as the author intended. Links to online resellers are available in our digital library. In addition, complete works may be ordered through an authorized reseller by filling out and returning to StudySync® the order form enclosed in this workbook.

Reading & Writing Companion   **25**

Skill:
Story Structure

Use the Checklist to analyze Story Structure in "American Horse." Refer to the sample student annotations about Story Structure in the text.

••• CHECKLIST FOR STORY STRUCTURE

In order to identify the choices an author makes when structuring specific parts of a text, note the following:

- ✓ the author's use of any literary devices, such as:

  - foreshadowing: a way of hinting at what will come later
  - flashback: a part of a story that shows something that happened in the past
  - pacing: how quickly or slowly the events of a story unfold
  - tension: a way of evoking emotion such as fear, stress, or anxiety in both the reader and the characters

- ✓ how the overall structure of the text contributes to its meaning as well as its aesthetic impact

  - the effect structure has on the impact it makes on the reader, such as the creation of suspense through the use of pacing
  - the use of flashback to reveal hidden dimensions of a character that affect the theme

To analyze how an author's choices concerning how to structure specific parts of a text contribute to its overall structure and meaning as well as its aesthetic impact, consider the following questions:

- ✓ How does the author structure the text overall? How does the author structure specific parts of the text?

- ✓ Does the author incorporate literary elements such as flashback or foreshadowing?

- ✓ How do these elements affect the overall text structure and the aesthetic impact of the text?

Skill:
Story Structure

Reread paragraphs 63–70 of "American Horse." Then, using the Checklist on the previous page, answer the multiple-choice questions below.

↻ YOUR TURN

1. The author uses a flashback to describes a memory that Albertine has about her father. What impact does this have on the reader and what does it reveal about Albertine's character?

   ○ A. The flashback reveals a memory of Albertine's father, which helps the reader better understand their relationship and shows how she is like her father.

   ○ B. The flashback reveals a memory of a dead butterfly, which helps the reader better understand how Albertine feels about death.

   ○ C. The flashback reveals an intimate experience between Albertine and her father, which reminds the reader of her humanity as well as her frailty and strength, despite her flaws and circumstances.

   ○ D. The flashback reveals a loving experience between Albertine and her father, which reminds the reader that she is like a butterfly who has been mistreated by society.

2. How does this flashback contribute to the overall meaning of the story?

   ○ A. The flashback captures the importance of dreams, memories, and the power of a mother.

   ○ B. The flashback captures the power of fathers, as well as the importance of the past.

   ○ C. The flashback captures the impact of memories on who we are, as well as the beauty of butterflies.

   ○ D. The flashback captures the importance of memories, human connections, and the power of familial love.

Skill:
Point of View

Use the Checklist to analyze Point of View in "American Horse." Refer to the sample student annotations about Point of View in the text.

••• CHECKLIST FOR POINT OF VIEW

In order to determine a narrator's point of view through what is directly stated is different from what is really meant, note the following:

✓ literary techniques intended to provide humor or criticism. Examples include:

- sarcasm, or the use of language that says one thing but means the opposite

- irony, or a contrast between what one expects to happen and what happens

- understatement, or an instance where a character deliberately makes a situation seem less important or serious than it is

- satire, or the use of humor, irony, exaggeration, or ridicule to expose and criticize people's foolishness or vices

✓ possible critiques an author might be making about contemporary society

✓ an unreliable narrator or character whose point of view cannot be trusted

To analyze a case in which grasping a point of view requires distinguishing what is directly stated in a text from what is really meant, consider the following questions:

✓ How does the cultural lens and experiences of the narrator or speaker shape his or her point of view? How does it shape what they say and how they say it?

✓ Is the narrator or speaker reliable? Why or why not?

✓ How does a character's or narrator's point of view contribute to a non-literal understanding of the text?

✓ How does the use of sarcasm, understatement, or satire add meaning to the story?

Skill:
Point of View

Reread paragraphs 55–61 of "American Horse." Then, using the Checklist on the previous page, answer the multiple-choice questions below.

⟲ YOUR TURN

1. This question has two parts. First, answer Part A. Then, answer Part B.

Part A: What is Harmony's motivation for speaking to Albertine the way that he does in this passage?

- ○ A. He wants to connect with her about their shared heritage in order to convince her to surrender peacefully.
- ○ B. He has already exhausted all other approaches, and this is his only remaining option.
- ○ C. Albertine has indicated that she will only negotiate with Harmony if he speaks respectfully to her.
- ○ D. Harmony is fearful of Albertine and what she is capable of doing to him.

Part B: Which line from the passage best supports your answer to Part A?

- ○ A. "But for godsakes, let's nobody get hurt. Come on out with the boy, why don't you? I know you got him in there."
- ○ B. "I ain't related to no pigs."
- ○ C. "He was a damn good man. I don't care what they say, Albertine, I knew him."
- ○ D. "Ma Cousin," he said in the Michif dialect that people used if they were relatives"

Close Read

Reread "American Horse." As you reread, complete the Skills Focus questions below. Then use your answers and annotations from the questions to help you complete the Write activity.

◎ SKILLS FOCUS

1. In *Invisible Man*, the narrator describes himself by wondering if he's a "phantom in other people's minds." Using details about the narrator from *Invisible Man* and about Albertine from paragraph 1 of "American Horse," compare the relationships among characterization, point of view, and thematic development in each text.

2. Identify a passage that describes Officer Brackett's thoughts about Vicki Koob. Analyze how Brackett's behaviors and underlying motivations contribute to a moral dilemma that influences the plot.

3. How does the structure the author uses to develop the setting contribute to the theme of the story?

4. Identify an instance in the text in which what a character says and what a character means are contradictory. How does this point of view add to your understanding of the story and its themes?

5. Each of the adults in this story believes he or she is doing what is right in the name of justice. Which adult do you believe is most motivated by justice and why? Support your answer with evidence from the text.

✎ WRITE

LITERARY ANALYSIS: Use your Skills Focus annotations and notes to clarify your understanding of the story structure in both *Invisible Man* and "American Horse." How does the way that each author structures the story help to develop similar themes about isolation? Use evidence from the text to support your analysis.

On Listening to Your Teacher Take Attendance

POETRY
Aimee Nezhukumatathil
2018

Introduction

Aimee Nezhukumatathil (b. 1974) was born in Chicago to a Filipina mother and an Indian father. She is the author of three collections of poetry and currently serves as a professor in the MFA program at the University of Mississippi. In this poem, Nezhukumatathil uses vivid imagery and detail to evoke the speaker's feelings as her last name is mispronounced by yet another teacher.

"... And when / everyone turns around to check out / your face, no need to flush red and warm."

1 Breathe deep even if it means you wrinkle
2 your nose from the fake-lemon **antiseptic**

3 of the mopped floors and wiped-down
4 doorknobs. The freshly soaped necks

5 and armpits. Your teacher means well,
6 even if he **butchers** your name like

7 he has a bloody sausage casing stuck
8 between his teeth, handprints

9 on his white, sloppy apron. And when
10 everyone turns around to check out

11 your face, no need to flush red and warm.
12 Just picture all the eyes as if your classroom

13 is one big scallop with its dozens of icy blues
14 and you will remember that winter your family

15 took you to the China Sea and you sank
16 your face in it to gaze at baby clams and sea stars

17 the size of your **outstretched** hand. And when
18 all those necks start to **crane**, try not to forget

19 someone once **lathered** their bodies, once patted them
20 dry with a fluffy towel after a bath, set out their clothes

21 for the first day of school. Think of their pencil cases
22 from third grade, full of sharp pencils, a pink pearl eraser.

23 Think of their handheld pencil sharpener and its tiny blade.

Aimee Nezhukumatathil, "On Listening to Your Teacher Take Attendance" from Oceanic. Copyright © 2018 by Aimee Nezhukumatathil. Used with the permission of The Permissions Company, Inc. on behalf of Copper Canyon Press, www.coppercanyonpress.org.

✏ WRITE

POETRY: Sometimes writing in the second person makes describing painful situations easier because it takes the focus off the speaker. The second person can also be used to give comfort, advice, or instruction to others. Using "On Listening to Your Teacher Take Attendance" as a guide, write a poem in the second person about a real or imagined situation in which the speaker describes personal memories, thoughts, or actions. Be sure to maintain the second-person voice and use figurative language throughout your poem.

Please note that excerpts and passages in the StudySync® library and this workbook are intended as touchstones to generate interest in an author's work. The excerpts and passages do not substitute for the reading of entire texts, and StudySync® strongly recommends that students seek out and purchase the whole literary or informational work in order to experience it as the author intended. Links to online resellers are available in our digital library. In addition, complete works may be ordered through an authorized reseller by filling out and returning to StudySync® the order form enclosed in this workbook.

Reading & Writing Companion

33

Civil Rights Act of 1964

INFORMATIONAL TEXT
Lyndon B. Johnson
with U.S. Congress
1964

Introduction

Easily the most memorable achievement of United States President Lyndon B. Johnson (1908–1973) was his role in the Civil Rights Act of 1964. Johnson famously signed the act into law, which banned discrimination based on race, national origin, religion, and gender in public places. The signing of this act also paved the way for Congress to pass the Voting Rights Act in 1965. Although the Civil Rights Act of 1964 was initially introduced during the presidency of Johnson's predecessor, John F. Kennedy, Johnson continued the fight against segregation in America in the wake of Kennedy's assassination. The following text includes the sections of the legislation that address the banning of discrimination in public places.

"All persons shall be entitled to be free, at any establishment or place, from discrimination . . ."

1   **SEC. 201.** (a) All persons shall be entitled to the full and equal enjoyment of the goods, services, facilities, and privileges, advantages, and accommodations of any place of public accommodation, as defined in this section, without **discrimination** or segregation on the ground of race, color, religion, or national origin.

Civil Rights Protest Clergy members stand in front as a crowd protesting for civil rights moves toward the Boston Common in Boston, April 23, 1965.

2   (b) Each of the following establishments which serves the public is a place of public accommodation within the meaning of this title if its operations affect commerce, or if discrimination or segregation by it is supported by State action:

3   (1) any inn, hotel, motel, or other establishment which provides lodging to **transient** guests, other than an establishment located within a building which contains not more than five rooms for rent or hire and which is actually occupied by the proprietor of such establishment as his residence;

4   (2) any restaurant, cafeteria, lunchroom, lunch counter, soda fountain, or other facility principally engaged in selling food for consumption on the premises, including, but not limited to, any such facility located on the premises of any retail establishment; or any gasoline station;

5   (3) any motion picture house,[1] theater, concert hall, sports arena, stadium or other place of exhibition or entertainment; and

6   (4) any establishment (A)(i) which is physically located within the premises of any establishment otherwise covered by this subsection, or (ii) within the premises of which is physically located any such covered establishment, and (B) which holds itself out as serving patrons of such covered establishment.

---

1. **motion picture house** a single-screen movie theater

7　(c) The operations of an establishment affect commerce within the meaning of this title if (1) it is one of the establishments described in paragraph (1) of subsection (b); (2) in the case of an establishment described in paragraph (2) of subsection (b), it serves or offers to serve interstate travelers or a **substantial** portion of the food which it serves, or gasoline or other products which it sells, has moved in commerce; (3) in the case of an establishment described in paragraph (3) of subsection (b), it customarily presents films, performances, athletic teams, exhibitions, or other sources of entertainment which move in commerce; and (4) in the case of an establishment described in paragraph (4) of subsection (b), it is physically located within the premises of, or there is physically located within its premises, an establishment the operations of which affect commerce within the meaning of this subsection. For purposes of this section, "commerce" means travel, trade, traffic, commerce, transportation, or communication among the several States, or between the District of Columbia and any State, or between any foreign country or any territory or possession and any State or the District of Columbia, or between points in the same State but through any other State or the District of Columbia or a foreign country.

8　(d) Discrimination or segregation by an establishment is supported by State action within the meaning of this title if such discrimination or segregation (1) is carried on under color of any law,[2] statute, ordinance, or regulation; or (2) is carried on under color of any custom or usage required or enforced by officials of the State or political subdivision thereof; or (3) is required by action of the State or political subdivision thereof.

9　(e) The provisions of this title shall not apply to a private club or other establishment not in fact open to the public, except to the extent that the facilities of such establishment are made available to the customers or patrons of an establishment within the **scope** of subsection (b).

10　**SEC. 202.** All persons shall be entitled to be free, at any establishment or place, from discrimination or segregation of any kind on the ground of race, color, religion, or national origin, if such discrimination or segregation is or purports to be required by any law, statute, ordinance, regulation, rule, or order of a State or any agency or political subdivision thereof.

11　**SEC. 203.** No person shall (a) withhold, deny, or attempt to withhold or deny, or deprive or attempt to deprive, any person of any right or privilege secured by section 201 or 202, or (b) intimidate, threaten, or coerce, or attempt to intimidate, threaten, or coerce any person with the purpose of interfering with

2. **under color of any law** with the appearance of legal power where it doesn't exist

any right or privilege secured by section 201 or 202, or (c) punish or attempt to punish any person for exercising or attempting to exercise any right or privilege secured by section 201 or 202.

https://www.eeoc.gov/eeoc/history/35th/thelaw/civil_rights_act.html

✏ WRITE

RESEARCH: The scope and specificity of the places named in this excerpt of the Civil Rights Act of 1964 serve not only to define the broad reach of the new law but also to recognize the particular battlegrounds where the fight for civil rights occurred. Research an event that took place in one of the locations mentioned in this portion of the Civil Rights Act of 1964. Then, write about how your research impacts your understanding of the text and the civil rights movement as a whole.

Please note that excerpts and passages in the StudySync® library and this workbook are intended as touchstones to generate interest in an author's work. The excerpts and passages do not substitute for the reading of entire texts, and StudySync® strongly recommends that students seek out and purchase the whole literary or informational work in order to experience it as the author intended. Links to online resellers are available in our digital library. In addition, complete works may be ordered through an authorized reseller by filling out and returning to StudySync® the order form enclosed in this workbook.

Reading & Writing
Companion

37

Second Inaugural Address

ARGUMENTATIVE TEXT
Abraham Lincoln
1865

Introduction

When newly elected President Abraham Lincoln (1809–1865) gave his first inaugural address, he promised to uphold the Union, even though the issue of slavery had already begun to tear apart the northern and southern states. Four years later, on March 4, 1865, nearing the end of a bitter Civil War, Lincoln stood again on the steps of the Capitol and delivered his second inaugural address. He used this opportunity to reflect upon the war, urge healing, and express hope for the future of the country.

"Fondly do we hope, fervently do we pray, that this mighty scourge of war may speedily pass away."

1   Fellow-Countrymen:

2   At this second appearing to take the oath of the Presidential office there is less occasion for an extended address than there was at the first. Then a statement somewhat in detail of a course to be **pursued** seemed fitting and proper. Now, at the expiration of four years, during which public

Civil War Soldiers Photograph of line of black civil war soldiers holding their rifles circa 1860.

declarations have been constantly called forth on every point and phase of the great contest which still absorbs the attention and engrosses the energies of the nation, little that is new could be presented. The progress of our arms, upon which all else chiefly depends, is as well known to the public as to myself, and it is, I trust, reasonably satisfactory and encouraging to all. With high hope for the future, no prediction in regard to it is **ventured**.

3   On the occasion corresponding to this four years ago all thoughts were anxiously directed to an impending civil war. All dreaded it, all sought to avert it. While the inaugural address was being delivered from this place, devoted altogether to saving the Union without war, insurgent agents were in the city seeking to destroy it without war—seeking to dissolve the Union and divide effects by negotiation. Both parties deprecated war, but one of them would make war rather than let the nation survive, and the other would accept war rather than let it perish, and the war came.

4   One-eighth of the whole population were colored slaves, not distributed generally over the Union, but localized in the southern part of it. These slaves **constituted** a peculiar and powerful interest. All knew that this interest was somehow the cause of the war. To strengthen, perpetuate, and extend this interest was the object for which the insurgents would rend the Union even

NOTES

Skill:
Primary and
Secondary Sources

This is definitely a primary source as it is a historical speech given at Lincoln's second inauguration. He is addressing the nation and immediately points out that the war is still a threat to the nation.

Copyright © BookheadEd Learning, LLC

Skill:
Arguments and
Claims

Lincoln appeals to both
ethos and pathos in
order to influence his
audience. He describes
how both sides pray to
the same God yet
places criticism on
those who ask God to
assist in the harm of
other Americans.

by war, while the Government claimed no right to do more than to restrict the territorial enlargement of it. Neither party expected for the war the magnitude or the duration which it has already **attained**. Neither anticipated that the cause of the conflict might cease with or even before the conflict itself should cease. Each looked for an easier triumph, and a result less fundamental and astounding. Both read the same Bible and pray to the same God, and each invokes His aid against the other. It may seem strange that any men should dare to ask a just God's assistance in wringing their bread from the sweat of other men's faces, but let us judge not, that we be not judged. The prayers of both could not be answered. That of neither has been answered fully. The Almighty has His own purposes. "Woe unto the world because of offenses; for it must needs be that offenses come, but woe to that man by whom the offense cometh." If we shall suppose that American slavery is one of those offenses which, in the providence of God, must needs come, but which, having continued through His appointed time, He now wills to remove, and that He gives to both North and South this terrible war as the woe due to those by whom the offense came, shall we discern therein any departure from those divine attributes which the believers in a living God always ascribe to Him? Fondly do we hope, fervently do we pray, that this mighty **scourge** of war may speedily pass away. Yet, if God wills that it continue until all the wealth piled by the bondsman's[1] two hundred and fifty years of unrequited toil shall be sunk, and until every drop of blood drawn with the lash[2] shall be paid by another drawn with the sword, as was said three thousand years ago, so still it must be said "the judgments of the Lord are true and righteous altogether."

Skill:
Informational
Text Elements

Lincoln concludes by
reflecting on the war in
an attempt to promote
forgiveness. While much
of the speech focused
on the divisiveness of
war, his conclusion
focuses on unity and
a desire to heal the
wounds and achieve
peace.

5 With **malice** toward none, with charity for all, with firmness in the right as God gives us to see the right, let us strive on to finish the work we are in, to bind up the nation's wounds, to care for him who shall have borne the battle and for his widow and his orphan, to do all which may achieve and cherish a just and lasting peace among ourselves and with all nations.

---

1. **bondsman** indentured servant or enslaved person
2. **lash** a whip, a means of intimidation or punishment against people who were indentured or enslaved

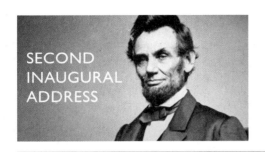

First Read

Read "Second Inaugural Address." After you read, complete the Think Questions below.

1. What do you think was Lincoln's main message in this inaugural address? Cite evidence from the text to support your response.

2. In the fourth paragraph, the word *interest* appears three times. What does *interest* refer to? Cite evidence from the text to support your response.

3. Lincoln mentions God and the Almighty a great deal toward the end of his speech. Does he believe that God is on the side of the North, the South, both, or neither? Cite evidence from the text to support your response.

4. Keeping in mind that the Latin root *-vent-* means "come," use context from the text to determine the meaning of the word **ventured** as it is used in paragraph 2. Write your definition of *venture* here and explain which clues helped you figure it out.

5. Use context clues to determine the meaning of the word **scourge** as it is used in paragraph 4. Write your definition of *scourge* here and explain which clues helped you figure it out.

Please note that excerpts and passages in the StudySync® library and this workbook are intended as touchstones to generate interest in an author's work. The excerpts and passages do not substitute for the reading of entire texts, and StudySync® strongly recommends that students seek out and purchase the whole literary or informational work in order to experience it as the author intended. Links to online resellers are available in our digital library. In addition, complete works may be ordered through an authorized reseller by filling out and returning to StudySync® the order form enclosed in this workbook.

Reading & Writing Companion **41**

Skill: Primary and Secondary Sources

Use the Checklist to analyze Primary and Secondary Sources in "Second Inaugural Address." Refer to the sample student annotations about Primary and Secondary Sources in the text.

••• CHECKLIST FOR PRIMARY AND SECONDARY SOURCES

In order to differentiate between primary and secondary sources, do the following:

✓ examine the source, noting the title, author, and date of publication

✓ identify the genre of the source

- Primary sources include letters, diaries, journals, speeches, eyewitness interviews, oral histories, memoirs, and autobiographies.
- Secondary sources include encyclopedia articles, newspaper and magazine articles, biographies, documentary films, history books, and textbooks.

If the source meets one or more of the following criteria, it is considered a primary source:

✓ original, first-hand account of an event or time period

✓ writing that takes place during the event or time period

If the source meets one or more of the following criteria, it is considered a secondary source:

✓ a book or an article that analyzes and interprets primary sources

✓ a second-hand account of a historical event

✓ a book or an article that interprets or analyzes creative work

To analyze seventeenth-, eighteenth-, and nineteenth-century foundational U.S. documents of historical and literary significance, consider the following questions:

✓ How is the source reliable and credible?

✓ What is the purpose of this source?

✓ What historical themes, such as patriotism or heroism, are brought out in the source?

✓ How does the author use anecdotes, interviews, allusions, or other rhetorical features?

✓ What gives this source literary or historical significance?

Skill: Primary and Secondary Sources

Reread paragraphs 4–5 of "Second Inaugural Address." Then, using the Checklist on the previous page, answer the multiple-choice questions below.

↻ YOUR TURN

1. Based on the context in this passage, what can you infer is the historical significance of this speech?

   ○ A. It is an example of how to make a strong, persuasive argument.
   ○ B. It marks the beginning of the nation's healing and reunification as well as the admittance of the sin of slavery.
   ○ C. It is a reminder to the Confederate states that they were to blame for the war.
   ○ D. It marks the end of the Civil War.

2. In the closing of this speech, the speaker addresses historical themes related to all of the following topics except:

   ○ A. war and peace
   ○ B. right and wrong
   ○ C. the will of God
   ○ D. international relations

Please note that excerpts and passages in the StudySync® library and this workbook are intended as touchstones to generate interest in an author's work. The excerpts and passages do not substitute for the reading of entire texts, and StudySync® strongly recommends that students seek out and purchase the whole literary or informational work in order to experience it as the author intended. Links to online resellers are available in our digital library. In addition, complete works may be ordered through an authorized reseller by filling out and returning to StudySync® the order form enclosed in this workbook.

Reading & Writing Companion   **43**

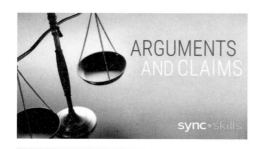

Skill:
Arguments and Claims

Use the Checklist to analyze Arguments and Claims in "Second Inaugural Address." Refer to the sample student annotations about Arguments and Claims in the text.

••• CHECKLIST FOR ARGUMENTS AND CLAIMS

In order to delineate the rhetorical appeals, premises, purposes, and arguments in works of public advocacy, note or do the following:

- ✓ the premise, or the basis of the proposal the individual or group makes, which is often based on logical reasoning and constitutional principles

- ✓ isolate the premise in a work of public advocacy

- ✓ determine whether the premise is based on logical reasoning and constitutional principles

- ✓ identify the purpose of the text and the position the writer takes

- ✓ Identify rhetorical appeals, including appeals to *logos* (logic), *ethos* (trust), and *pathos* (emotions)

To evaluate the rhetorical appeals, premises, purposes, and arguments in works of public advocacy, consider the following questions:

- ✓ What rhetorical appeals does the writer use? What effect do these appeals have on the audience?

- ✓ What position does the writer take?

- ✓ How does the writer use legal reasoning to support his or her position?

- ✓ In a work of public advocacy, how does the individual or group try to influence or support a cause or policy?

Skill:
Arguments and Claims

Reread paragraph 4 of "Second Inaugural Address." Then, using the Checklist on the previous page, answer the multiple-choice questions below.

⟳ YOUR TURN

1. Which answer best outlines the structure of the argument in paragraph 4?

   ○ A. evidence, reasons, appeals, call to action
   ○ B. historical background, thesis, evidence, appeals, conclusion
   ○ C. conclusion, historical background, and call to action
   ○ D. thesis, background, conclusion, call to action

2. Which sentence contains rhetorical appeals?

   ○ A. One-eighth of the whole population were colored slaves, not distributed generally over the Union, but localized in the southern part of it.
   ○ B. These slaves constituted a peculiar and powerful interest.
   ○ C. To strengthen, perpetuate, and extend this interest was the object for which the insurgents would rend the Union even by war, while the Government claimed no right to do more than to restrict the territorial enlargement of it.
   ○ D. Neither anticipated that the cause of the conflict might cease with or even before the conflict itself should cease.

Please note that excerpts and passages in the StudySync® library and this workbook are intended as touchstones to generate interest in an author's work. The excerpts and passages do not substitute for the reading of entire texts, and StudySync® strongly recommends that students seek out and purchase the whole literary or informational work in order to experience it as the author intended. Links to online resellers are available in our digital library. In addition, complete works may be ordered through an authorized reseller by filling out and returning to StudySync® the order form enclosed in this workbook.

Reading & Writing Companion   45

Skill:
Informational Text Elements

Use the Checklist to analyze Informational Text Elements in "Second Inaugural Address." Refer to the sample student annotations about Informational Text Elements in the text.

••• CHECKLIST FOR INFORMATIONAL TEXT ELEMENTS

In order to identify a complex set of ideas or sequence of events, note the following:

✓ key details in the text that provide information about individuals, events, and ideas

✓ interactions between specific individuals, ideas, or events

✓ important developments of ideas over the course of the text

✓ transition words and phrases that signal interactions between individuals, events, and ideas, such as *because, as a consequence,* or *as a result.*

✓ similarities and differences of types of information in a text

✓ visual text elements such as photos, graphs, or charts, that support ideas in the text or enhance the reader's understanding

To analyze a complex set of ideas or sequence of events and explain how specific individuals, ideas, or events interact and develop over the course of the text, consider the following questions:

✓ How does the author present the information as a sequence of events?

✓ How does the order in which ideas or events are presented affect the connections between them?

✓ How do specific individuals, ideas, or events interact and develop over the course of the text?

✓ What other features, if any, help readers to analyze the events, ideas, or individuals in the text?

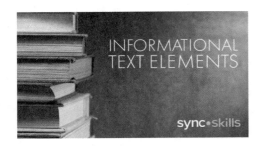

Skill:
Informational Text Elements

Reread paragraph 4 of "Second Inaugural Address." Then, using the Checklist on the previous page, answer the multiple-choice questions below.

⟳ YOUR TURN

1. What key ideas and important events are used to support the development of the central idea that the Civil War was God's divine retribution for allowing slavery?

   ○ A. Lincoln makes the claim that the cause of the war was slavery and then develops the central idea by pointing out that neither side understood the magnitude of the war nor its impact.

   ○ B. Lincoln makes the claim that the cause of the war was slavery and then develops the central idea by referencing ideas and events from the Bible to make the point that the war was God's will in response to the inhumanity of slavery.

   ○ C. Lincoln makes the claim that the cause of the war was slavery and then develops the central idea by pointing out that slavery was only happening in the South and therefore God would punish the South.

   ○ D. Lincoln makes the claim that the cause of the war was slavery and then develops the central idea that prayers on both sides could not be answered and that both the North and the South had to endure this terrible war.

2. What does the use of the transition word "yet" indicate about the relationship between the ideas that precede it and those in the final sentence of this paragraph?

   ○ A. The word "yet" highlights the similarities between the cruelty of slavery and the cruelty of war.

   ○ B. The word "yet" highlights the contrast between how those who believe in God feel toward the war and how those who don't believe in God feel toward the war.

   ○ C. The word "yet" emphasizes Lincoln's desire for the war to end as quickly as possible.

   ○ D. The word "yet" highlights the contrast between the strong desire for the war to end, and the acceptance that the war was necessary because it was God's will.

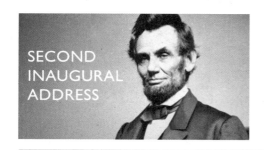

Close Read

Reread "Second Inaugural Address." As you reread, complete the Skills Focus questions below. Then use your answers and annotations from the questions to help you complete the Write activity.

◎ SKILLS FOCUS

1. How does Lincoln establish credibility with his audience? What information does he include to prove he is knowledgeable on this subject? Support your answer with evidence from the text.

2. Highlight a passage from paragraph 4 that reveals Lincoln's message. What is Lincoln's claim, or thesis, in his "Second Inaugural Address"?

3. Highlight the passage that contains Lincoln's conclusion. Is his conclusion convincing? Why or why not?

4. To what extent does Lincoln believe that the Civil War was necessary in order to create a more just nation? Support your answer with evidence from the text.

✏ WRITE

RHETORICAL ANALYSIS: In his "Second Inaugural Address," Lincoln acknowledges the horror of the Civil War, the human cost on both sides, and the damage the war has caused the nation. He also very clearly and powerfully takes a side. Identify the claim that is integral to Lincoln's speech. Then, analyze how Lincoln orders and develops his ideas in order to support his claim. Evaluate how effective Lincoln was in supporting his main argument. Support your response with textual evidence.

I've Been to the Mountaintop

ARGUMENTATIVE TEXT
Martin Luther King Jr.
1968

Introduction

Dr. Martin Luther King Jr. (1929–1968) delivered "I've Been to the Mountaintop" at Mason Temple in Memphis, Tennessee on April 3, 1968. King had been to Memphis a number of times in the spring of 1968 to show his support for African American sanitation workers who were striking to protest unfair working conditions. On March 29, the situation in Memphis exploded when looters broke away from a protest march led by King and vandalized businesses on Beale Street. Chaos ensued, resulting in injuries, arrests, and the death of one man. Devastated by the violence, King returned to Memphis several days later to refocus the campaign on nonviolence and the plight of the sanitation workers. "I've Been to the Mountaintop" was King's last speech. He was assassinated on the evening of April 4, 1968, outside of his room at the Lorraine Motel in Memphis.

"We have an opportunity to make America a better nation."

1   Thank you very kindly, my friends. As I listened to Ralph Abernathy[1] in his eloquent and generous introduction and then thought about myself, I wondered who he was talking about. It's always good to have your closest friend and associate to say something good about you. And Ralph Abernathy is the best friend that I have in the world.

2   I'm delighted to see each of you here tonight in spite of a storm warning. You reveal that you are determined to go on anyhow. Something is happening in Memphis; something is happening in our world.

3   And you know, if I were standing at the beginning of time, with the possibility of taking a kind of general and panoramic view of the whole of human history up to now, and the Almighty said to me, "Martin Luther King, which age would you like to live in?" I would take my mental flight by Egypt and I would watch God's children in their magnificent **trek** from the dark dungeons of Egypt through or rather across the Red Sea, through the wilderness on toward the promised land.[2] And in spite of its magnificence, I wouldn't stop there. I would move on by Greece and take my mind to Mount Olympus.[3] And I would see Plato, Aristotle, Socrates, Euripides and Aristophanes[4] assembled around the Parthenon, and I would watch them around the Parthenon,[5] as they discussed the great and eternal issues of reality.

4   But I wouldn't stop there. I would go on, even to the great hey-day of the Roman Empire. And I would see **developments** around there, through various emperors and leaders. But I wouldn't stop there. I would even come up to the

---

1. **Ralph Abernathy** Civil rights leader Ralph Abernathy (1926–1990) was a mentor to Dr. King, and his successor as president of the Southern Christian Leadership Conference.
2. **"through the wilderness on toward the promised land"** a reference to the Book of Numbers in the Old Testament, in which the Israelites are made to wander in the wilderness for forty years before reaching their destination
3. **Mount Olympus** the highest mountain in Greece and the mythical residence of the Greek gods
4. **Plato, Aristotle, Socrates, Euripides and Aristophanes** great ancient Greek philosophers and playwrights, and the founders of Western thought
5. **Parthenon** 5th century BCE temple on the Acropolis dedicated to the goddess Athena and dominating central Athens

NOTES

day of the Renaissance, and get a quick picture of all that the Renaissance did for the cultural and esthetic life of man. But I wouldn't stop there. I would even go by the way that the man for whom I am named had his habitat. And I would watch Martin Luther as he tacked his ninety-five theses[6] on the door at the church of Wittenberg.

5   But I wouldn't stop there. I would come on up even to 1863, and watch a **vacillating** President by the name of Abraham Lincoln finally come to the conclusion that he had to sign the Emancipation Proclamation. But I wouldn't stop there. I would even come up to the early thirties, and see a man grappling with the problems of the bankruptcy of his nation. And come with an eloquent cry that we have nothing to fear but fear itself.

6   But I wouldn't stop there. Strangely enough, I would turn to the Almighty, and say, "If you allow me to live just a few years in the second half of the Twentieth Century, I will be happy." Now that's a strange statement to make, because the world is all messed up. The nation is sick. Trouble is in the land. Confusion all around. That's a strange statement. But I know, somehow, that only when it is dark enough can you see the stars. And I see God working in this period of the Twentieth Century in a way that men, in some strange way, are responding—something is happening in our world. The masses of people are rising up. And wherever they are assembled today, whether they are in Johannesburg, South Africa; Nairobi, Kenya; Accra, Ghana; New York City; Atlanta, Georgia; Jackson, Mississippi; or Memphis, Tennessee—the cry is always the same—"We want to be free."

7   Another reason that I'm happy to live in this period is that we have been forced to a point where we are going to have to grapple with the problems that men have been trying to grapple with through history, but the demands didn't force them to do it. Survival demands that we grapple with them. Men, for years now, have been talking about war and peace. But now, no longer can they just talk about it. It is no longer a choice between violence and nonviolence in this world, it's nonviolence or nonexistence.

8   That is where we are today. And also in the human rights revolution, if something isn't done, and done in a hurry, to bring the colored peoples of the world out of their long years of poverty, their long years of hurt and neglect, the whole world is doomed. Now, I'm just happy that God has allowed me to live in this period to see what is unfolding. And I'm happy that He's allowed me to be in Memphis.

⚙ Skill: Language, Style, and Audience

Grapple is used three times and this repetition intensifies the call to action as survival now depends on it. This engages the audience and the serious tone suggests that choosing not to act peacefully could lead to nonexistence.

6. **ninety-five theses** proposals by theologian Martin Luther (1483–1546) which began the Protestant split from the Catholic Church

Copyright © BookheadEd Learning, LLC

Skill: Central or
Main Idea

*King's main idea is
introduced here. He is
strongly stating that all
people are God's
children and should be
treated equally. All
human beings deserve
to be treated decently
and he is determined to
make this happen.*

9   I can remember, I can remember when Negroes were just going around as Ralph has said so often, scratching where they didn't itch, and laughing when they were not tickled. But that day is all over. We mean business now, and we are determined to gain our rightful place in God's world.

10 And that's all this whole thing is about. We aren't engaged in any negative protest and in any negative arguments with anybody. We are saying that we are determined to be men. We are determined to be people. We are saying that we are God's children. And if we're God's children, we don't have to live like we are forced to live.

11 Now, what does all of this mean in this great period of history? It means that we've got to stay together. We've got to stay together and maintain unity. You know, whenever Pharaoh wanted to prolong the period of slavery in Egypt, he had a favorite, favorite formula for doing it. What was that? He kept the slaves fighting among themselves. But whenever the slaves get together, something happens in Pharaoh's court, and he cannot hold the slaves in slavery. When the slaves get together, that's the beginning of getting out of slavery. Now let us maintain unity.

12 Secondly, let us keep the issues where they are. The issue is injustice. The issue is the refusal of Memphis to be fair and honest in its dealings with its public servants, who happen to be sanitation workers. Now we've got to keep attention on that. That's always the problem with a little violence. You know what happened the other day, and the press dealt only with the window breaking. I read the articles. They very seldom got around to mentioning the fact that one thousand, three hundred sanitation workers are on strike, and that Memphis is not being fair to them, and that Mayor Loeb is in dire need of a doctor. They didn't get around to that.

13 Now we're going to march again, and we've got to march again, in order to put the issue where it is supposed to be. And force everybody to see that there are thirteen hundred of God's children here suffering, sometimes going hungry, going through dark and dreary nights wondering how this thing is going to come out. That's the issue. And we've got to say to the nation, "We know how it's coming out." For when people get caught up with that which is right and they are willing to sacrifice for it, there is no stopping point short of victory.

14 We aren't going to let any mace stop us. We are masters in our nonviolent movement in disarming police forces; they don't know what to do. I've seen them so often. I remember in Birmingham, Alabama, when we were in that majestic struggle there we would move out of the 16th Street Baptist Church

NOTES

day after day, by the hundreds we would move out. And Bull Connor[7] would tell them to send the dogs forth, and they did come; but we just went before the dogs singing, "Ain't gonna let nobody turn me 'round." Bull Connor next would say, "Turn the fire hoses on." And as I said to you the other night, Bull Connor didn't know history. He knew a kind of physics that somehow didn't relate to the transphysics that we knew about. And that was the fact that there was a certain kind of fire that no water could put out. And we went before the fire hoses; we had known water. If we were Baptist or some other denominations, we had been immersed. If we were Methodist, and some others, we had been sprinkled, but we knew water.

15 That couldn't stop us. And we just went on before the dogs and we would look at them; and we'd go on before the water hoses and we would look at it, and we'd just go on singing "Over my head I see freedom in the air." And then we would be thrown in the paddy wagons, and sometimes we were stacked in there like sardines in a can. And they would throw us in, and old Bull would say, "Take them off," and they did; and we would just go in the paddy wagon singing, "We Shall Overcome." And every now and then we'd get in jail, and we'd see the jailers looking through the windows being moved by our prayers, and being moved by our words and our songs. And there was a power there which Bull Connor couldn't adjust to; and so we ended up transforming Bull into a steer, and we won our struggle in Birmingham.

16 Now we've got to go on in Memphis just like that. I call upon you to be with us when we go out Monday. Now about injunctions: We have an injunction and we're going into court tomorrow morning to fight this illegal, unconstitutional injunction. All we say to America is, "Be true to what you said on paper." If I lived in China or even Russia, or any totalitarian country, maybe I could understand some of these illegal injunctions. Maybe I could understand the denial of certain basic First Amendment privileges, because they hadn't committed themselves to that over there. But somewhere I read of the freedom of assembly. Somewhere I read of the freedom of speech. Somewhere I read of the freedom of press. Somewhere I read that the greatness of America is the right to protest for right. And so just as I say, we aren't going to let any dog or water hose turn us around, we aren't going to let any injunction turn us around. We are going on.

17 We need all of you. And you know what's beautiful to me, is to see all of these ministers of the Gospel. It's a marvelous picture. Who is it that is supposed to articulate the longings and aspirations of the people more than the preacher? Somehow the preacher must have a kind of fire shut up in his bones. And

Skill: Rhetoric

King establishes credibility—uses ethos—by describing his persistence and victory in Birmingham, even in face of extreme adversity. He uses ethos to persuade the audience to continue their nonviolent protests in Memphis.

---

7. **Bull Connor** Theophilus Eugene 'Bull' Connor (1897–1973) was Commissioner of Public Safety of Birmingham, Alabama, when he ordered the use of attack dogs and fire hoses against civil rights demonstrators in May of 1963

whenever injustice is around he must tell it. Somehow the preacher must be an Amos, and say, "When God speaks who can but prophesy?" Again with Amos,[8] "Let justice roll down like waters and righteousness like a mighty stream." Somehow the preacher must say with Jesus, "The Spirit of the Lord is upon me, because He hath anointed me to deal with the problems of the poor."

18   And I want to commend the preachers, under the leadership of these noble men: James Lawson, one who has been in this struggle for many years; he's been to jail for struggling; he's been kicked out of Vanderbilt University for this struggle, but he's still going on, fighting for the rights of his people. Reverend Ralph Jackson, Billy Kiles. I could just go right on down the list, but time will not permit. But I want to thank all of them. And I want you to thank them, because so often, preachers aren't concerned about anything but themselves. And I'm always happy to see a relevant ministry.

19   It's all right to talk about "long white robes over yonder,"[9] in all of its symbolism. But ultimately people want some suits and dresses and shoes to wear down here! It's all right to talk about "streets flowing with milk and honey,"[10] but God has commanded us to be concerned about the slums down here, and his children who can't eat three square meals a day. It's all right to talk about the New Jerusalem,[11] but one day, God's preacher must talk about the new New York, the new Atlanta, the new Philadelphia, the new Los Angeles, the new Memphis, Tennessee. This is what we have to do.

20   Now the other thing we'll have to do is this. Always anchor our external direct action with the power of economic withdrawal. Now, we are poor people. Individually, we are poor when you compare us with white society in America. We are poor. Never stop and forget, that collectively, that means all of us together, collectively, we are richer than all the nations in the world, with the exception of nine. Did you ever think about that? After you leave the United States, Soviet Russia, Great Britain, West Germany, France, and I could name the others, the American Negro collectively is richer than most nations of the world. We have an annual income of more than thirty billion dollars a year, which is more than all of the exports of the United States, and more than the national budget of Canada. Did you know that? That's power right there, if we know how to pool it.

---

8. **Amos** one of the twelve prophets of the Old Testament

9. **"long white robes over yonder"** a reference to the belief in an afterlife in heaven as reward for earthly suffering

10. **"streets flowing with milk and honey"** in the Old Testament, God promised Abraham the land of Canaan (Israel) would "flow with milk and honey"

11. **New Jerusalem** in the Old Testament, Ezekiel says that there will one day be a New Jerusalem as capital of God's kingdom on Earth

21 We don't have to argue with anybody. We don't have to curse and go around acting bad with our words. We don't need any bricks and bottles, we don't need any Molotov cocktails. We just need to go around to these stores, and to these massive industries in our country, and say, "God sent us by here to say to you that you're not treating his children right. And we've come here to ask you to make the first item on your agenda—fair treatment where God's children are concerned. Now if you are not prepared to do that, we do have an agenda that we must follow. And our agenda calls for withdrawing economic support from you."

22 And so far, as a result of this, we are asking you tonight, to go out and tell your neighbors not to buy Coca-Cola in Memphis. Go by and tell them not to buy Sealtest Milk. Tell them not to buy—what is the other bread?—Wonder Bread. And what is the other bread company, Jesse? Tell them not to buy Hart's Bread. As Jesse Jackson has said, "Up to now, only the garbage men have been feeling pain, now we must kind of redistribute the pain." We are choosing these companies because they haven't been fair in their hiring policies; and we are choosing them because they can begin the **process** of saying they are going to support the needs and the rights of these men who are on strike. And then they can move downtown and tell Mayor Loeb to do what is right.

23 But not only that, we've got to strengthen black institutions. I call upon you to take your money out of the banks downtown and deposit your money in Tri-State Bank. We want a "bank-in" movement in Memphis. Go by the Savings and Loan Association. I'm not asking you something that we don't do ourselves at SCLC. Judge Hooks and others will tell you that we have an account here in the savings and loan association from the Southern Christian Leadership Conference. We are telling you to follow what we are doing. Put your money there. You have six or seven black insurance companies here in the city of Memphis. Take out your insurance there. We want to have an "insurance-in."

24 Now these are some practical things that we can do. We begin the process of building a greater economic **base**. And at the same time, we are putting pressure where it really hurts. I ask you to follow through here.

25 Now, let me say as I move to my conclusion, that we've got to give ourselves to this struggle until the end. Nothing would be more tragic than to stop at this point, in Memphis. We've got to see it through. And when we have our march, you need to be there. If it means leaving work, if it means leaving school—be there. Be concerned about your brother. You may not be on strike. But either we go up together, or we go down together.

NOTES

26   Let us develop a kind of dangerous unselfishness. One day a man came to Jesus; and he wanted to raise some questions about some vital matters of life. At points, he wanted to trick Jesus, and show him that he knew a little more than Jesus knew, and through this throw him off base. Now that question could have easily ended up in a philosophical and theological debate. But Jesus immediately pulled that question from mid-air, and placed it on a dangerous curve between Jerusalem and Jericho. And he talked about a certain man, who fell among thieves. You remember that a Levite and a priest passed by on the other side. They didn't stop to help him. And finally a man of another race came by. He got down from his beast, decided not to be compassionate by proxy. But he got down with him, administered first aid, and helped the man in need. Jesus ended up saying, "This was the good man, this was the great man, because he had the capacity to project the 'I' into the 'thou,' and to be concerned about his brother" Now you know, we use our imagination a great deal to try to determine why the priest and the Levite didn't stop. At times we say they were busy going to a church meeting— an ecclesiastical gathering—and they had to get on down to Jerusalem so they wouldn't be late for their meeting. At other times we would speculate that there was a religious law that "One who was engaged in religious ceremonials was not to touch a human body twenty-four hours before the ceremony." And every now and then we begin to wonder whether maybe they were not going down to Jerusalem, or down to Jericho, rather to organize a "Jericho Road Improvement Association." That's a possibility. Maybe they felt that it was better to deal with the problem from the causal root, rather than to get bogged down with an individual effect.

27   But I'm going to tell you what my imagination tells me. It's possible that those men were afraid. You see, the Jericho road is a dangerous road. I remember when Mrs. King and I were first in Jerusalem. We rented a car and drove from Jerusalem down to Jericho. And as soon as we got on that road, I said to my wife, "I can see why Jesus used this as the setting for his parable." It's a winding, meandering road. It's really conducive for ambushing. You start out in Jerusalem, which is about 1200 miles, or rather 1200 feet above sea level. And by the time you get down to Jericho, fifteen or twenty minutes later, you're about 2200 feet below sea level. That's a dangerous road. In the days of Jesus it came to be known as the "Bloody Pass." And you know, it's possible that the priest and the Levite looked over that man on the ground and wondered if the robbers were still around. Or it's possible that they felt that the man on the ground was merely faking. And he was acting like he had been robbed and hurt, in order to seize them over there, lure them there for quick and easy seizure. And so the first question that the Priest asked, the first question that the Levite asked was, "If I stop to help this man, what will happen to me?" But then the Good Samaritan came by. And he reversed the question: "If I do not stop to help this man, what will happen to him?"

28 That's the question before you tonight. Not, "If I stop to help the sanitation workers, what will happen to my job." Not, "If I stop to help the sanitation workers what will happen to all of the hours that I usually spend in my office every day and every week as a pastor?" The question is not, "If I stop to help this man in need, what will happen to me?" The question is, "If I do not stop to help the sanitation workers, what will happen to them?" That's the question.

29 Let us rise up tonight with a greater readiness. Let us stand with a greater determination. And let us move on in these powerful days, these days of challenge to make America what it ought to be. We have an opportunity to make America a better nation. And I want to thank God, once more, for allowing me to be here with you.

30 You know, several years ago, I was in New York City autographing the first book that I had written. And while sitting there autographing books, a demented black woman came up. The only question I heard from her was, "Are you Martin Luther King?"

31 And I was looking down writing, and I said, "Yes." And the next minute I felt something beating on my chest. Before I knew it I had been stabbed by this demented woman. I was rushed to Harlem Hospital. It was a dark Saturday afternoon. And that blade had gone through, and the X-rays revealed that the tip of the blade was on the edge of my aorta, the main artery. And once that's punctured, you drown in your own blood—that's the end of you.

32 It came out in the *New York Times* the next morning, that if I had merely sneezed, I would have died. Well, about four days later, they allowed me, after the operation, after my chest had been opened, and the blade had been taken out, to move around in the wheel chair in the hospital. They allowed me to read some of the mail that came in, and from all over the states and the world, kind letters came in. I read a few, but one of them I will never forget. I had received one from the President and the Vice-President. I've forgotten what those telegrams said. I'd received a visit and a letter from the Governor of New York, but I've forgotten what that letter said. But there was another letter that came from a little girl, a young girl, who was a student at the White Plains High School. And I looked at that letter, and I'll never forget it. It said simply, "Dear Dr. King, I am a ninth-grade student at the White Plains High School." She said, "While it should not matter, I would like to mention that I'm a white girl. I read in the paper of your misfortune, and of your suffering. And I read that if you had sneezed, you would have died. And I'm simply writing you to say that I'm so happy that you didn't sneeze."

33 And I want to say tonight—I want to say tonight that I, too, am happy that I didn't sneeze. Because if I had sneezed, I wouldn't have been around here in 1960, when students all over the South started sitting-in at lunch counters.

Skill: Central or Main Idea

Achieving King's goal of universal equality will require determination and unity, two ideas that are emphasized through much of the speech. Here, he asks his audience to rise and stand together to demand equality.

Skill:
Rhetoric

King uses the same repeating phrase to emphasize and memorialize the successes of the civil rights movement. The repetition of these accomplishments serves to persuade the audience that victory is possible and to keep fighting.

And I knew that as they were sitting in, they were really standing up for the best in the American dream. And taking the whole nation back to those great wells of democracy which were dug deep by the Founding Fathers in the Declaration of Independence and the Constitution. If I had sneezed, I wouldn't have been around here in 1961, when we decided to take a ride for freedom, and ended segregation in interstate travel. If I had sneezed, I wouldn't have been around here in 1962, when Negroes in Albany, Georgia decided to straighten their backs up. And whenever men and women straighten their backs up, they are going somewhere, because a man can't ride your back unless it is bent. If I had sneezed, if I had sneezed, I wouldn't have been here in 1963, when the black people of Birmingham, Alabama aroused the conscience of this nation, and brought into being the Civil Rights Bill. If I had sneezed, I wouldn't have had a chance later that year, in August, to try to tell America about a dream that I had had. If I had sneezed, I wouldn't have been down in Selma, Alabama, to see the great movement there. If I had sneezed, I wouldn't have been in Memphis to see a community rally around those brothers and sisters who are suffering. I'm so happy that I didn't sneeze.

34   And they were telling me, now, it doesn't matter, now. It really doesn't matter what happens now. I left Atlanta this morning, and as we got started on the plane, there were six of us, the pilot said over the public address system, "We are sorry for the delay, but we have Dr. Martin Luther King on the plane. And to be sure that all of the bags were checked, and to be sure that nothing would be wrong on the plane, we had to check out everything carefully. And we've had the plane protected and guarded all night."

35   And then I got into Memphis. And some began to say the threats, or talk about the threats that were out. What would happen to me from some of our sick white brothers?

36   Well, I don't know what will happen now. We've got some difficult days ahead. But it really doesn't matter with me now, because I've been to the mountaintop. And I don't mind. Like anybody, I would like to live a long life. Longevity has its place. But I'm not concerned about that now. I just want to do God's will. And He's allowed me to go up to the mountain. And I've looked over. And I've seen the Promised Land. I may not get there with you. But I want you to know tonight that we, as a people, will get to the promised land. And I'm happy tonight. I'm not worried about anything. I'm not fearing any man. Mine eyes have seen the glory of the coming of the Lord.

@ 1968 Dr. Martin Luther King, Jr. © renewed 1996 Coretta Scott King.

First Read

Read "I've Been to the Mountaintop." After you read, complete the Think Questions below.

☁ THINK QUESTIONS

1. What is "this whole thing about," according to the speaker? Cite evidence from paragraph 10 to support your answer.

2. What specific actions does the speaker propose the audience take in order to exercise their "power of economic withdrawal"? Support you answer with evidence from the text.

3. Citing evidence from the text to support your answer, explain why the speaker tells the parable of the Good Samaritan in "I've Been to the Mountaintop."

4. What is the meaning of the word **vacillating** as it is used in the text? Write your best definition here, along with a brief explanation of how you arrived at its meaning.

5. Read the following dictionary entry:

base
base /bās/ *noun*

1. the bottom part of something that provides structural support
2. any one of the four stations in a softball or baseball infield
3. something from which people draw support

Use context to determine which of these definitions most closely matches the use of **base** in the text. Write the correct definition of *base* here and explain how you figured it out.

Copyright © BookheadEd Learning, LLC

Skill:
Rhetoric

Use the Checklist to analyze Rhetoric in "I've Been to the Mountaintop." Refer to the sample student annotations about Rhetoric in the text.

••• CHECKLIST FOR RHETORIC

In order to identify a speaker's reasoning, point of view, and use of evidence and rhetoric, note the following:

- ✓ the stance, or position, the speaker takes on a topic

- ✓ the use of rhetorical appeals including appeals to *logos* (logic), *ethos* (trust), and *pathos* (emotions)

- ✓ the use of rhetorical devices, such as:

  - sensory language that appeals to the senses and creates a vivid picture in the minds of readers and listeners

  - repetition of the same word or phrase to emphasize an idea or claim. Look for:

    - > anaphora, or repetition at the start of a sentence or clause

    - > anadiplosis, or repetition of last word in a sentence or clause

- ✓ the speaker's choice of words, the points he or she chooses to emphasize, and the tone, or general attitude

To evaluate a speaker's point of view, reasoning, and use of evidence and rhetoric, consider the following questions:

- ✓ What is the speaker's point of view? Is their stance based on sound, logical reasoning? Why or why not?

- ✓ Does the author use facts and evidence to make a point? Are they exaggerated? How do you know?

- ✓ Does the speaker use rhetorical devices? If so, are they effective? Why or why not?

- ✓ What points does the speaker choose to emphasize? How does the speaker's choice of words affect his or her tone?

Skill:
Rhetoric

Reread paragraphs 3–6 of "I've Been to the Mountaintop." Then, using the Checklist on the previous page, answer the multiple-choice questions below.

⟳ YOUR TURN

1. The speaker repeats the phrase "I wouldn't stop there" seven times in paragraphs 3–6. This rhetorical device is called —

   ○ A. the rhetorical appeal known as *pathos*.
   ○ B. anaphora.
   ○ C. rhetorical shift.
   ○ D. antithesis.

2. Which statement best describes the effect of the rhetorical device in Question 1 on how the passage is read and understood?

   ○ A. It powerfully calls attention to the progress of human history while creating a personal connection between the speaker and his audience that is intended to convince listeners that remarkable progress is yet to come right there in Memphis.
   ○ B. It reveals that the speaker will soon move on and that the people must commit to carrying on his nonviolent approach to reaching equality for all.
   ○ C. It alerts listeners to the fact that the speaker knows a lot about history and they should be honored that he has come back to Memphis to help fight for workers' rights and civil rights nationwide.
   ○ D. It tells listeners that they should be wary of participating in marches or protests as they are likely to be part of only one small moment in history.

3. The speaker says, "But I know, somehow, that only when it is dark enough can you see the stars." Why does the speaker use the rhetorical device evident in this sentence?

   ○ A. He uses it to change the audience's focus from the historic times he mentioned to the importance of the march that is to take place the next day.
   ○ B. He uses it as a way to logically defend the troubled times in the United States and around the world.
   ○ C. He uses it to help convince the audience to fight for civil rights by describing a figurative contrast between keeping hope in the troubled times they live in.
   ○ D. He uses it to provide proof that nonviolent protests are not always effective and therefore not necessary.

Skill:
Central or Main Idea

Use the Checklist to analyze Central or Main Idea in "I've Been to the Mountaintop." Refer to the sample student annotations about Central or Main Idea in the text.

••• CHECKLIST FOR CENTRAL OR MAIN IDEA

In order to identify two or more central ideas of a text, note the following:

✓ the main idea in each paragraph or group of paragraphs

✓ key details in each paragraph or section of text, distinguishing what they have in common

✓ whether the details contain information that could indicate more than one main idea in a text

- A science text, for example, may provide information about a specific environment and also a message on ecological awareness.

- A biography may contain equally important ideas about a person's achievements, influence, and the time period in which the person lives or lived.

✓ when each central idea emerges

✓ ways that the central ideas interact and build on one another

To determine two or more central ideas of a text and analyze their development over the course of the text, including how they interact and build on one another to provide a complex analysis, consider the following questions:

✓ What main idea(s) do the details in each paragraphs explain or describe?

✓ What central or main ideas do all the paragraphs support?

✓ How do the central ideas interact and build on one another? How is that affected by when they emerge?

✓ How might you provide an objective summary of the text? What details would you include?

Skill:
Central or Main Idea

Reread paragraphs 34–36 of "I've Been to the Mountaintop." Then, using the Checklist on the previous page, answer the multiple-choice questions below.

⟳ YOUR TURN

1. How does sharing the threats he has received in this passage help King add to one of the central ideas of the text?

   ○ A. It helps the reader understand that Dr. King is in grave danger and could be harmed.
   ○ B. It strengthens his argument that the path to equality won't be easy, but that it is worth it.
   ○ C. It builds on of the themes of unity and opportunity even in times of instability.
   ○ D. It helps strengthen his argument that equal rights should be granted to all Americans.

2. What is the central idea of King's closing paragraph?

   ○ A. That regardless of what happens next, Dr. King has seen what could be and has faith in God that one day African Americans will achieve equality.
   ○ B. That the Promised Land is a place that all African Americans will get to no matter what as King has already been there.
   ○ C. That African Americans should come together to make the world a better place.
   ○ D. That nothing matters to Dr. King now as he has been to the mountaintop and feels that he is now free.

Please note that excerpts and passages in the StudySync® library and this workbook are intended as touchstones to generate interest in an author's work. The excerpts and passages do not substitute for the reading of entire texts, and StudySync® strongly recommends that students seek out and purchase the whole literary or informational work in order to experience it as the author intended. Links to online resellers are available in our digital library. In addition, complete works may be ordered through an authorized reseller by filling out and returning to StudySync® the order form enclosed in this workbook.

Reading & Writing
Companion

63

Skill: Language, Style, and Audience

Use the Checklist to analyze Language, Style, and Audience in "I've Been to the Mountaintop." Refer to the sample student annotations about Language, Style, and Audience in the text.

••• CHECKLIST FOR LANGUAGE, STYLE, AND AUDIENCE

In order to determine an author's style and possible intended audience, do the following:

- ✓ identify instances where the author uses key terms throughout the course of a text

- ✓ examine surrounding words and phrases to determine the context, connotation, style, and tone of the term

- ✓ analyze how the author's treatment of the key term affects the reader's understanding of the text

- ✓ note the audience—both intended and unintended—and possible reactions to the author's word choice, style, and treatment of key terms

To analyze how an author's treatment of language and key terms affect the reader's understanding of the text, consider the following questions:

- ✓ How do the author's word choices enhance or change what is being described?

- ✓ How do the author's word choices affect the reader's understanding of key terms and ideas in the text?

- ✓ How do choices about language affect the author's style and audience?

- ✓ How often does the author use this term or terms?

Skill: Language, Style, and Audience

Reread paragraphs 32 and 33 of "I've Been to the Mountaintop." Then, using the Checklist on the previous page, answer the multiple-choice questions below.

↻ YOUR TURN

1. How does the repetition of the phrase "if I had sneezed" enhance the meaning of these paragraphs?

   ○ A. It emphasizes that King is proud of all of the work that he has done.

   ○ B. It enhances the reader's understanding of how King felt happy to be alive.

   ○ C. It emphasizes that King was part of many great moments in the Civil Rights struggle which he would have missed had he sneezed.

   ○ D. It enhances the reader's understanding of the impact of the events that occured over the years.

2. What is the effect of this summary of successes on the audience?

   ○ A. It reminds the audience of the gradual progress that has been made which inspires action, hope and the need to keep fighting.

   ○ B. It teaches the audience about the major events of the civil rights movement.

   ○ C. It helps the reader understand how close King was to dying and how happy he is to be alive.

   ○ D. It builds tension by foreshadowing King's assassination.

Please note that excerpts and passages in the StudySync® library and this workbook are intended as touchstones to generate interest in an author's work. The excerpts and passages do not substitute for the reading of entire texts, and StudySync® strongly recommends that students seek out and purchase the whole literary or informational work in order to experience it as the author intended. Links to online resellers are available in our digital library. In addition, complete works may be ordered through an authorized reseller by filling out and returning to StudySync® the order form enclosed in this workbook.

Reading & Writing Companion

65

Close Read

Reread "I've Been to the Mountaintop." As you reread, complete the Skills Focus questions below. Then use your answers and annotations from the questions to help you complete the Write activity.

◎ SKILLS FOCUS

1. What is one of King's central or main ideas in this text? Support your answer with textual evidence. (Use paragraph 6 "But I know... to be free" as the highlighted text)

2. Identify a passage in "I've Been to the Mountaintop" that reveals the audience of the speech. Analyze how King communicates his purpose to this audience.

3. Highlight a rhetorical device that King uses in his speech. Then, analyze the effect of the rhetorical devices have on the way the text is read and understood.

4. Identify an example in the text where King urges his audience to partake in non-violent forms of resistance. Explain why you believe nonviolence is important for King in the fight for equality.

✎ WRITE

RHETORICAL ANALYSIS: What makes rhetoric effective? Identify King's main idea and purpose in this speech. Then, discuss what aspect of King's rhetoric is most crucial to convincing his audience of his main idea. Cite examples of rhetoric from the text and explain how it is used to support King's central idea.

The Night Before Christmas

FICTION
Tomás Rivera
2015

Introduction

Tomás Rivera (1935–1984) was a notable poet, author, and educator. A migrant worker early in his life and the first in his family to graduate from high school, Rivera earned a PhD from the University of Oklahoma and is recognized for his significant contributions to Chicano literature. In "The Night Before Christmas," an immigrant mother struggles to make Christmas special in the face of both financial and mental obstacles. As the story attests, in spite of the common hopes that most American families share, the holidays do not look the same in every family.

"Aren't we good like the other kids?"

Note: Please be advised that the following text contains mild profanity.

1   Christmas Eve was **approaching** and the barrage of commercials, music and Christmas cheer over the radio and the blare of announcements over the loud speakers on top of the station wagon advertising movies at the Teatro Ideal resounded and seemed to draw it closer. It was three days before Christmas when Doña María decided to buy something for her children. This was the first time she would buy them toys. Every year she intended to do it but she always ended up facing up to the fact that, no, they couldn't afford it. She knew that her husband would be bringing each of the children candies and nuts anyway and so she would **rationalize** that they didn't need to get them anything else. Nevertheless, every Christmas the children asked for toys. She always appeased them with the same promise. She would tell them to wait until the sixth of January, the day of the Reyes Magos,[1] and by the time that day arrived the children had already forgotten all about it. But now she noticed that each year the children seemed less and less taken with Don Chon's visit on Christmas Eve when he came bearing a sack of oranges and nuts.

2   "But why doesn't Santa Claus bring us anything?"

3   "What do you mean? What about the oranges and nuts he brings you?"

4   "No, that's Don Chon."

5   "No, I'm talking about what you always find under the sewing machine."

6   "What, Dad's the one who brings that, don't think we don't know that. Aren't we good like the other kids?"

7   "Of course, you're good children. Why don't you wait until the day of the Reyes Magos. That's when toys and gifts really arrive. In Mexico, it's not Santa Claus who brings gifts, but the Three Wise Men. And they don't come until the sixth of January. That's the real date."

**Skill:
Story Elements**

The dialogue reveals that Doña María is upset about not being able to buy gifts for her children. She tells them to wait, but gifts never come. This hints at the developing conflict and the stress of being impoverished.

---

1. **Reyes Magos**   the traveling characters from the story of the birth of Christ, known in English as the Three Wise Men, the Three Kings, or the Magi

NOTES

8   "Yeah, but they always forget. They've never brought us anything, not on Christmas Eve, not on the day of the Three Kings."

9   "Well, maybe this time they will."

10   "Yeah, well, I sure hope so."

11   That was why she made up her mind to buy them something. But they didn't have the money to spend on toys. Her husband worked almost eighteen hours a day washing dishes and cooking at a restaurant. He didn't have time to go downtown and buy toys. Besides, they had to save money every week to pay for the trip up north. Now they even charged for children too, even if they rode standing up the whole way to Iowa. So it cost them a lot to make the trip. In any case, that night when her husband arrived, tired from work, she talked to him about getting something for the children.

12   "Look, Viejo,[2] the children want something for Christmas."

13   "What about the oranges and nuts I bring them?"

14   "Well, they want toys. They're not content anymore with just fruits and nuts. They're a little older now and more aware of things."

15   "They don't need anything."

16   "Now, you can't tell me you didn't have toys when you were a kid."

17   "I used to make my own toys, out of clay . . . little horses and little soldiers . . . "

18   "Yes, but it's different here. They see so many things . . . come on, let's go get them something . . . I'll go to Kress myself."

19   "You?"

20   "Yes, me." "Aren't you afraid to go downtown? You remember that time in Wilmar, out in Minnesota, how you got lost downtown. Are you sure you're not afraid?"

21   "Yes, yes, I remember, but I'll just have to get my courage up. I've thought about it all day long and I've set my mind to it. I'm sure I won't get lost here. Look, I go out to the street. From here you can see the ice house. It's only four blocks away, so Doña Regina tells me. When I get to the ice house I turn to the right and go two blocks and there's downtown. Kress is right there. Then,

---

2. **Viejo** (slang) old man; one's father

⚙ Skill:
Story Elements

The dialogue reveals the mother's fear about going downtown alone. Her husband questions her decision, indicating that she has had negative experiences going downtown alone before. This sets up the climax of the story.

NOTES

I come out of Kress, walk back towards the ice house and turn back on this street, and here I am."

22　"I guess it really won't be difficult. Yeah. Fine. I'll leave you some money on top of the table when I go to work in the morning. But be careful, Vieja, there's a lot of people downtown these days."

23　The fact was that Doña María very rarely left the house. The only time she did was when she visited her father and her sister who lived on the next block. And she only went to church whenever someone died and, occasionally, when there was a wedding. But she went with her husband, so she never took notice of where she was going. And her husband always brought her everything. He was the one who bought the groceries and clothing. In reality she was unfamiliar with downtown even though it was only six blocks away. The cemetery was on the other side of downtown and the church was also in that direction. The only time that they passed through downtown was whenever they were on their way to San Antonio or whenever they were returning from up north. And this would usually be during the wee hours of the morning or at night. But that day she was **determined** and she started making preparations. The next day she got up early as usual, and after seeing her husband and children off, she took the money from the table and began getting ready to go downtown. This didn't take her long.

24　"My God, I don't know why I'm so fearful. Why, downtown is only six blocks from here. I just go straight and then after I cross the tracks turn right. Then go two blocks and there's Kress. On the way back, I walk two blocks back and then I turn to the left and keep walking until I'm home again. God willing, there won't be any dogs on the way. And I just pray that the train doesn't come while I'm crossing the tracks and catches me right in the middle . . . I just hope there's no dogs . . . I hope there's no train coming down the tracks."

25　She walked the distance from the house to the railroad tracks rapidly. She walked down the middle of the street all the way. She was afraid to walk on the sidewalk. She feared she might get bitten by a dog or that someone might grab her. In fact, there was only one dog along the entire stretch and most of the people didn't even notice her walking toward downtown. She nevertheless kept walking down the middle of the street and, luckily, not a single car passed by, otherwise she would not have known what to do. Upon arriving at the crossing she was suddenly struck by intense fear. She could hear the sound of moving trains and their whistles blowing and this was unnerving her. She was too scared to cross. Each time she mustered enough courage to cross she heard the whistle of the train and, frightened, she retreated and ended up at the same place. Finally, overcoming her fear, she shut her eyes and crossed the tracks. Once she got past the tracks, her fear began to **subside**. She got to the corner and turned to the right.

26   The sidewalks were crowded with people and her ears started to fill up with a ringing sound, the kind that, once it started, it wouldn't stop. She didn't recognize any of the people around her. She wanted to turn back but she was caught in the flow of the crowd which shoved her onward toward downtown and the sound kept ringing louder and louder in her ears. She became frightened and more and more she was finding herself unable to remember why she was there amid the crowd of people. She stopped in an alley way between two stores to regain her composure a bit. She stood there for a while watching the passing crowd.

27   "My God, what is happening to me? I'm starting to feel the same way I did in Wilmar. I hope I don't get worse. Let me see . . . the ice house is in that direction no it's that way. No, my God, what's happening to me? Let me see . . . I came from over there to here. So it's in that direction. I should have just stayed home. Uh, can you tell me where Kress is, please? . . . Thank you."

28   She walked to where they had pointed and entered the store. The noise and pushing of the crowd was worse inside. Her anxiety soared. All she wanted was to leave the store but she couldn't find the doors anywhere, only stacks and stacks of merchandise and people crowded against one another. She even started hearing voices coming from the merchandise. For a while she stood, gazing blankly at what was in front of her. She couldn't even remember the names of the things. Some people stared at her for a few seconds, others just pushed her aside. She remained in this state for a while, then she started walking again. She finally made out some toys and put them in the bag. Suddenly she no longer heard the noise of the crowd. She only saw the people moving about their legs, their arms, their mouths, their eyes. She finally asked where the door, the exit was. They told her and she started in that direction. She pressed through the crowd, pushing her way until she pushed open the door and exited. She had been standing on the sidewalk for only a few seconds, trying to figure out where she was, when she felt someone grab her roughly by the arm. She was grabbed so tightly that she gave out a cry.

29   "Here she is . . . these damn people, always stealing something, stealing. I've been watching you all along. Let's have that bag."

30   "But . . . "

31   Then she heard nothing for a long time. All she saw was the pavement moving swiftly towards her face and a small pebble that bounced into her eye and was hurting a lot. She felt someone pulling her arms and when they turned her, face up, all she saw were faces far away. Then she saw a security guard with a gun in his holster and she was terrified. In that instant she thought about her children and her eyes filled with tears. She started crying. Then she

lost consciousness of what was happening around her, only feeling herself drifting in a sea of people, their arms brushing against her like waves.

32 "It's a good thing my **compadre** happened to be there. He's the one who ran to the restaurant to tell me. How do you feel?"

33 "I think I must be crazy, Viejo."

34 "That's why I asked you if you weren't afraid you might get sick like in Wilmar."

35 "What will become of my children with a mother who's insane? A crazy woman who can't even talk, can't even go downtown."

36 "Anyway, I went and got the notary public. He's the one who went with me to the jail. He explained everything to the official. That you got dizzy and that you get nervous attacks whenever you're in a crowd of people."

37 "And if they send me to the insane asylum? I don't want to leave my children. Please, Viejo, don't let them take me, don't let them. I shouldn't have gone downtown."

38 "Just stay here inside the house and don't leave the yard. There's no need for it anyway. I'll bring you everything you need. Look, don't cry anymore, don't cry. No, go ahead and cry, it'll make you feel better. I'm gonna talk to the kids and tell them to stop bothering you about Santa Claus. I'm gonna tell them there's no Santa Claus, that way they won't trouble you with that anymore."

39 "No, Viejo, don't be mean. Tell them that if he doesn't bring them anything on Christmas Eve, it's because the Reyes Magos will be bringing them something."

40 "But . . . well, all right, whatever you say. I suppose it's always best to have hope."

41 The children, who were hiding behind the door, heard everything, but they didn't quite understand it all. They awaited the day of the Reyes Magos as they did every year. When that day came and went with no arrival of gifts, they didn't ask for explanations.

"The Night Before Christmas" is reprinted with permission from the publisher of "...y no se lo trago la tierra/ . . . And the Earth Did Not Devour Him" by Tomas Rivera (© 1987 Arte Público Press—University of Houston)

First Read

Read "The Night Before Christmas." After you read, complete the Think Questions below.

1. Describe the main character in the short story. Be specific, and make sure to support your response with details from the text.

2. What does Doña María mean when she says to her husband, "Yes, but it's different here. They see so many things"? Cite evidence from the story in your explanation.

3. How do you think Doña María views the world outside her house? Explain, citing evidence from the text.

4. How do you think Doña María views the world outside her house? Explain, citing evidence from the text.

5. The word **subside** comes from the Latin word *subsidere*, which means "to sit down or to sink." With this in mind and using context from the text, write your own definition of *subside* as it is used in this short story and explain how you came to your conclusion.

Please note that excerpts and passages in the StudySync® library and this workbook are intended as touchstones to generate interest in an author's work. The excerpts and passages do not substitute for the reading of entire texts, and StudySync® strongly recommends that students seek out and purchase the whole literary or informational work in order to experience it as the author intended. Links to online resellers are available in our digital library. In addition, complete works may be ordered through an authorized reseller by filling out and returning to StudySync® the order form enclosed in this workbook.

Reading & Writing Companion   **73**

Skill:
Story Elements

Use the Checklist to analyze Story Elements in "The Night Before Christmas." Refer to the sample student annotations about Story Elements in the text.

••• CHECKLIST FOR STORY ELEMENTS

In order to identify the impact of the author's choices regarding how to develop and relate elements of a story or drama, note the following:

- ✓ where and when the story takes place, who the main characters are, and the main conflict, or problem, in the plot

- ✓ the order of the action

- ✓ how the characters are introduced and developed

- ✓ how dialogue is used to develop the characters and the plot

- ✓ the impact that the author's choice of setting has on the characters and their attempt to solve the problem

- ✓ the point of view the author uses, and how this shapes what readers know about the characters in the story

To analyze the impact of the author's choices regarding how to develop and relate elements of a story or drama, consider the following questions:

- ✓ How do the author's choices affect the story elements? The development of the plot?

- ✓ How does the setting influence the characters?

- ✓ Which elements of the setting impact the plot, and in particular the problem the characters face and must solve? How does this contribute to the theme?

- ✓ How does the author introduce and develop characters in the story? Why do you think they made these choices?

- ✓ What does dialogue reveal about the characters?

Skill:
Story Elements

Reread paragraphs 27–30 of "The Night Before Christmas." Then, using the Checklist on the previous page, answer the multiple-choice questions below.

⟳ YOUR TURN

1. How does the internal dialogue in paragraph 28 intensify the conflict?

   ○ A. It reveals that Doña María has trouble with directions which causes her to get lost.

   ○ C. It reveals that Doña María is scared, which causes her to get lost in Kress.

   ○ D. It reveals that Doña María's husband was right as she gets lost and is unable to get gifts for her children.

2. How does the description of the setting in paragraph 29 impact the climax of the story?

   ○ A. The description of Doña María's experience in the crowded store leads to her being grabbed by a security guard.

   ○ B. The description of Doña María's experience in the crowded store leads to her getting lost in the store and fainting.

   ○ C. The description of Doña María's experience in the crowded store leads to her to not be able to hear.

   ○ D. The description of Doña María's experience in the crowded store leads to her being accused of stealing which causes her to faint.

Please note that excerpts and passages in the StudySync® library and this workbook are intended as touchstones to generate interest in an author's work. The excerpts and passages do not substitute for the reading of entire texts, and StudySync® strongly recommends that students seek out and purchase the whole literary or informational work in order to experience it as the author intended. Links to online resellers are available in our digital library. In addition, complete works may be ordered through an authorized reseller by filling out and returning to StudySync® the order form enclosed in this workbook.

Reading & Writing Companion   75

Close Read

Reread "The Night Before Christmas." As you reread, complete the Skills Focus questions below. Then use your answers and annotations from the questions to help you complete the Write activity.

◎ SKILLS FOCUS

1. Identify how the main character in the story is introduced. Explain how the reader's understanding of Doña María changes over the course of the story.

2. Find a detail about the setting of the story. How does the setting of the story influence the characters or plot?

3. Throughout the story, the characters reference what has happened on other occasions when Doña María has gone out alone. Identify one such instance. Explain what impact the mention of this event has on the reader.

4. Identify how Doña María describes herself in the story. Do you agree with her description? Why or why not?

5. This text highlights different marginalized groups who are often victims of injustice. Choose one group represented in this story and explain what aspects of the story would need to change to ensure justice for all. Support your answer with evidence from the text.

✏ WRITE

LITERARY ANALYSIS: How does Tomás Rivera use dialogue to shape what you know about his characters? How does dialogue affect the plot of the story? What insight does the dialogue in this story provide the reader and what is its impact? In a written response, analyze the author's use of dialogue in this short story. Cite evidence from the text to support your analysis.

The Last Ride of Cowboy Bob

INFORMATIONAL TEXT
Skip Hollandsworth
2005

Introduction

In "The Last Ride of Cowboy Bob" the acclaimed journalist and editor Skip Hollandsworth (b. 1957) recounts the infamous Texan bank robber known to the FBI as Cowboy Bob—and to her family and friends as the beautiful, free-spirited Peggy Jo. For a dozen or so months in the early 90s, Peggy Jo Tallas confounded federal agents and bank tellers with meticulously planned heists in which she approached cashiers wearing her cowboy costume and slid them a note that read

"She was very skilled and very efficient, as good as any man I've ever come across."

NOTES

> Note: The following text has been edited or altered due to length.

1   Peggy Jo Tallas was, by all accounts, the classic good-hearted Texas woman. For much of her adult life, she lived with her **ailing** mother in a small apartment in the Dallas suburbs. Every morning, after waking up and making her bed, always taking the time to smooth out all the wrinkles in the sheets with her hands, she'd walk into her mother's bedroom. She'd wrap a robe around her mother's shoulders, lead her to the kitchen, fix her cereal, and lay out her pills. For a few minutes, the two of them would sit at the table, making small talk. Peggy Jo, who didn't like to eat until later in the day, would often smoke a cigarette and drink Pepsi out of a coffee cup. Then, after her mother was finished eating, Peggy Jo would gently guide her back to her bedroom, prop a pillow behind her head, set a glass of tap water and her romance novel on the side table, and walk back into her own room to get dressed.

2   Usually, she liked wearing khaki pants, a simple blouse, and loafers. But on a lovely morning in May 1991, Peggy Jo, who was then 46 years old, decided to wear something different. She walked over to her dresser, the top of which held a few small glass sculptures of dolphins with **iridescent** eyes that she had been collecting off and on for more than a decade. She opened one of the lower drawers and pulled out a pair of men's pants and a dark men's shirt. From her closet, she grabbed a men's brown leather jacket that she kept on a hanger. She then reached for a Styrofoam mannequin's head that was on a shelf in the closet. A fake beard was pinned to it and on top was a white cowboy hat.

3   She took off her nightshirt and put on the clothes along with some boots that were too big for her feet. She stuffed a towel under her shirt to make herself look heavier. She stepped into the bathroom, rubbed some adhesive across her face, pasted on the fake beard, and colored her hair with gray paint she had bought at a costume shop. She placed the cowboy hat on her head, put on a large pair of silver-rimmed sunglasses, and pulled on a pair of gloves. She then took a few minutes to write a note on a sheet of lined paper and put it in her pocket.

4   "Be back in a minute," Peggy Jo told her mother, tiptoeing past her room. She walked outside, got behind the wheel of her 1975 two-door Pontiac Grand Prix, drove to the American Federal Bank just off West Airport Freeway in Irving, pulled into the parking lot, stepped into the bank's lobby, and headed toward the counter, where a young female teller was smiling cheerfully.

5   "Hello, sir," the teller said. "How may I help you?"

6   Peggy Jo pulled out the note she had written. "This is a bank robbery," it read. "Give me your money. No marked bills or dye packs."

7   The stunned teller handed over a stack of cash from her drawer. Peggy Jo nodded, stuck the money into a satchel, and walked out of the bank. She then drove straight back to her apartment, where her mother was still in bed, getting hungry, hoping Peggy Jo would return soon to fix her lunch.

8   In the criminology textbooks, they are invariably described as products of a deprived socioeconomic background. Most of them are young male drug addicts who don't have the slightest idea what they are doing. When they burst into banks, their fingers twitch and their heads swivel back and forth as they look for security guards. They shout out threats and wave guns in the air. When they get their money, they run madly for the exits, bowling over anyone in their path, and they squeal away in their cars, leaving tire tracks on the road.

9   And then there was Peggy Jo Tallas. "I promise you, my Aunt Peggy was the last person on earth you would ever imagine robbing a bank," said her niece, Michelle. "Whenever I was in a car with her, she never drove above the speed limit. If anything, she drove below it. And she always came to a complete stop at stop signs."

10 But Peggy Jo didn't just rob a bank. Beginning with that May 1991 trip to American Federal, she robbed lots of banks. According to the FBI, she was one of the most unusual bank robbers of her generation, a modern-day Bonnie without a Clyde[1] who always worked alone, never using a partner to operate as her lookout or drive her getaway car. She was also a master of disguise, her cross-dressing outfits so carefully designed that law enforcement officials, studying bank surveillance tapes, had no idea they were chasing a woman. What's more, she was so determined not to hurt anyone that she never carried a weapon into any bank she robbed. "I have to admit, I admired her style," said Steve Powell, a former FBI agent who spent most of his thirty-year career chasing bank robbers and who supervised bank robbery investigations for the Dallas office of the FBI in the early nineties. "She knew

1. **Bonnie without a Clyde** Bonnie Parker and Clyde Barrow were a notorious Depression-era outlaw couple who embarked on a crime spree across the central United States

NOTES

how to get in and out of a bank in sixty seconds. She was very skilled and very efficient, as good as any man I've ever come across."

11 Although female bank robbers are not unheard of—it is estimated that women commit less than 5 percent of the some 7,600 bank robberies that take place each year in the United States—almost all of them are young women who, like most of the men, rob banks for drug money. And only a few of those women rob more than a bank or two before they quit or get caught. Accordingly, when Powell and his team of FBI agents happened to corner Peggy Jo near her apartment in 1992, they assumed they would never be dealing with her again. She was one of those women, they believed, who had **succumbed** to a strange bout of middle-aged craziness. She wasn't poor. She wasn't an addict or an alcoholic. And from what people who knew her said, she was utterly harmless—"A sweet lady who once chatted with me about the best way to grow plants on the front porch," one neighbor noted. Seemingly **repentant**, Peggy Jo pleaded guilty to bank robbery and quietly went off to prison for almost three years. And that seemed to be that.

12 But then, this past May, the story broke that a small bank in the East Texas city of Tyler had been robbed by a sixty-year-old woman. The woman was dressed in black, wearing a black wide-brimmed hat and dark sunglasses that covered much of her face. She was polite and did not use a gun when she confronted the teller. She placed the money she received in a black satchel, nodded "thank you," walked out the door, and climbed into a twenty-foot Frontier RV with pretty purple shades around the windows. She turned on the ignition, pushed on the gas pedal, and headed south on Texas Highway 69, straight out of town.

13 After all those years, Peggy Jo Tallas had returned.

From *Texas Monthly*, November 2005. Used by permission of *Texas Monthly*.

✏ WRITE

RESEARCH: For all the notoriety of her crimes, Peggy Jo "received a mild, 33-month sentence." Do you think Peggy Jo deserved a more severe punishment or a more lenient one? Research the standard minimum and maximum sentencing for bank robberies in America. What circumstances typically factor into sentencing and how does Peggy Jo's strange case deviate from the norm? Cite specific evidence from the text to support your argument.

The Four Foods

FICTION
Dalia Rosenfeld
2017

Introduction

Dalia Rosenfeld is the award-winning author of the short story collection *The Worlds We Think We Know*. Her work has has been published by the *Michigan Quarterly Review* and *The Atlantic*, among other places. She currently lives in Israel, where she teaches writing at Bar Ilan University. Her story "The Four Foods" humorously explores the fraught relationship between an imposing scholar of Judaism and his adult daughter who tries to close the distance between them

"Together my father and I chew. We chew and chew and chew."

1   My father is an **imposing** man. Small, with dark, sad eyes and gums that bleed when he brushes them in the morning. I ask my mother why he scares me so much. "It's his knowledge," she says. "He knows things."

2   I go out and buy a dictionary. I go out and buy textual sources for the study of world religions. History. Philosophy. The natural sciences. I craft concepts into sentences, theories into questions best asked over the telephone. I call my father. I say, "Dad?"

3   My mother tells me not to call him so often. "You're distracting him from his writing," she says. "Call me instead."

4   I cry into the phone. "You're so easy, and he's so hard."

5   "Now, honey." My mother tries to comfort me. "Now, pussycat."

6   We meet for lunch, my father and I. We sit across from each other like retirees and squint at the specials written in pink chalk above the counter.

7   Midway through our sandwiches we begin to talk. "Mom says she's allergic to goose feathers," I say. "What are you going to do with all the pillows from Europe?"

8   My father takes a sip of water. "Those pillows belonged to your great-grandmother. The feathers in them came all the way from Lvov."

9   I nod. "It's the **shtetl**. Mom doesn't want to go back."

10   My father sucks up a sesame seed through a gap between his teeth, and I wait for him to acknowledge my analysis. For years, the pillows have reminded my mother that she has not always been an American. Now she is starting to sneeze whenever she gets near them.

11   "There is no shtetl anymore. There is no going back," my father says.

12 "But **figuratively**, the Old World—" That evening, my mother scolds me over the phone. "There is no figuratively," she says. "Why do you always have to blab about what you don't know?"

13 "I thought we could talk about Europe or something—what it means to us."

14 "To us?"

15 "As Jews."

16 My mother thinks for a moment, then says, "Some Jews have allergies to feathers. I happen to be one of them. Burden your father with something else."

17 I sit in my apartment and stare at the wall. Through it I hear a brief hammering, then a silence, and then someone knocking at my door. I cannot pretend that it is anyone but Jake.

18 "Can you help me out a minute?" he says, pointing in the direction of his door, two pairs of bunny ears hanging from the toes of his house slippers.

19 While he nails a poster of Christie Brinkley to the wall, I lend Jake my eye. "Left," I say. "Left—OK, now right." "Like this?" "If it has to be." I try to take the encounter at face value. I try to subtract the hammer and the house slippers and the bikini behind the glass, and see Jake for the ordinary man he is. "The picture looks good," I say.

20 Jake opens the refrigerator and pulls out a carton of milk. He drinks. "What do you have on your walls?" I stare at the ring of milk above his mouth. "I'm waiting for just the right thing. A family picture, perhaps. Or maybe a picture of just my father, sitting at his typewriter. I would blow it up really big, and hang it in my living room." Jake puts down the milk carton. "Are you serious?"

21 I imagine my father sitting at his typewriter, whacking at the keys with **agitated** fingers. I have never actually seen him do this; the door to his study is always closed. "Maybe I would put it in the bathroom," I say, reconsidering.

22 "My father can only work in complete solitude." My parents have me over for dinner. We sit around the kitchen table like a family and pass things: the salad, the bread, the soup bowls to be filled and then refilled. My father pours himself a glass of wine for his heart and asks, "Leah, have you been jogging lately?"

23 "I made a few rounds this morning," I say. "And I was thinking, if Leonard Bernstein was Jewish, why did he write a Mass?"

24   My father stares at his reflection in the soup. "I really don't know, honey."

25   I wait for more, but nothing comes. "Of course you know," I say. "You just don't feel like thinking when I'm around." My mother deflects a frown by raising a napkin to her lips. "Leonard Bernstein is dead," she says firmly. "There's nothing to think about." She lowers the napkin and frowns anyway. I turn to my father. He looks tired. A nerve twitches at his neck whenever he swallows, as though keeping time to some silent music. My father sees me looking and says, "You think a lot about Jews, don't you?"

26   I shrug. "I guess it runs in the family." My father has written many books, all of them about Jews.

27   "How about thinking about the family instead?" my mother suggests.

28   I want to explain to my father that I am trying to do just that, but he is already immersed in other, more intimate concerns, his eyes looking right at me but without registering a thing. Mahler's conversion to Catholicism? The expulsion from Spain? 1933? I am losing him. Again. Still. I call my mother. I say, "It's not his knowledge. It's something else."

29   "It's *your* knowledge," my mother agrees. "It gets in the way."

30   "My knowledge? What do I know?"

31   "Nothing," my mother agrees. "That's the problem."

32   I go out and attend lectures, study forms and functions, foundations and first principles. I take notes while watching television. It is not a joke, I don't laugh. Usually I cry.

33   My mother calls me in the midst of it all. "Your father is in the hospital," she says. "He's got a hernia."

34   "Was it me?" I ask.

35   "It wasn't me," my mother says. I visit my father in the hospital. He is lying in a small white bed in a small white room divided by a curtain. The nurse has parted his hair on the wrong side. My mother tells me to leave the curtain drawn; a very sick man is lying on the other side, and the separation will do my father good.

36   I look at my father, open my mouth, then close it again. My mother takes over. "How are you feeling, Howard?" My father sticks out his tongue. "Ugh," he says. I have never heard my father say ugh before. I repeat it. "Ugh?" My

mother pretends to smooth out a wrinkle in my father's sheet, and pinches me. "Ow!" I squeal.

37   My father opens his eyes a little wider. "Ow?" Soon the nurse comes in to serve lunch. She places a plastic tray wrapped in aluminum foil on my father's lap, then disappears behind the curtain. I sit at the edge of my father's bed and remove the foil. Together we study the four **compartments**: chicken, broccoli, pears, water.

38   There is so much I want to say to my father at this moment, but I'm not sure where to begin, especially with my mother standing over me, at the ready. At the very least I want to tell him how good he looks in his hospital gown, like one of the high priests of the Temple in Jerusalem, before it was destroyed.

39   "You look good, Dad," I say, blinking away everything in the room but the robe. I am close enough to feel that it is cotton. "Like one of the *kohanim* in the *Beit Hamikdash*."[1]

40   I give my father a few seconds to answer, and when he doesn't, pick up the fork on his tray and slide it under a piece of chicken.

41   "What are you doing, Leah?" My mother tries to stop me, but I push her away. During visiting hours he is as much mine as anyone else's. Carefully I reach over and place the chicken into my father's mouth.

42   My father takes the food between his lips. He chews and chews and chews. "How is the food, Howard?" my mother asks, still thinking I am flubbing it all up. "Is it too salty?" Before he can answer, I break off two more pieces of chicken with my fingers. One piece I gently push into my father's mouth; the second piece I put into my own.

43   Together my father and I chew. We chew and chew and chew.

44   When we can chew no more, I look at my father and wait for a signal.

45   "*Nu*, how's the food, you pigs?" my mother asks again.

46   We swallow; my father belches. The stripes of his gown ripple under his raised belly.

47   Together we say, "Mmm."

---

1. **"one of the *kohanim* in the *Beit Hamikdash*"** one of the hereditary Jewish priests of the first temple on Jerusalem's Temple Mount

✏ WRITE

PERSONAL RESPONSE: Can you relate to the narrator's misunderstandings with her father? How much has your awareness of cultural or familial traditions been shaped, either actively or passively, by an older generation? Do you differ in the way you interpret those traditions? Are there particular traditions that bring you and your family together? Write a personal response in which you compare and contrast your experiences with those of the narrator and her father in "The Four Foods." Use personal anecdotes as well as evidence from the text in your response.

Gaman

POETRY
Christine Kitano
2016

Introduction

Christine Kitano is a celebrated Japanese and Korean American poet, as well as a professor of creative writing, poetry, and Asian American literature. Her works include the poetry collections *Sky Country* and *Birds of Paradise*. The title of her poem "*Gaman*" means "to endure, persist, or persevere" in Japanese. In this poem, the speaker explores her family history through the eyes of her grandmother who immigrated to the United States from Japan only to have her family's life torn apart when her son, Kitano's father, was sent to an internment

"For the sake of the children, / we'll teach them to forgive the fears of others,"

1 It was night when the buses stopped.
2 It was too dark to see the road,

3 or if there was a road. So we waited.
4 We watched. We thought of back home,

5 how the orchards would swell with fruit,
6 how the trees would strain, then give way

7 under their **ripe** weight. The pockmarked
8 moon the face of an apple, pitted

9 with rot. But of course not. Someone
10 would **intervene**, would make of our absence

11 a profit. When we came, the boat, anchored
12 at San Francisco Bay, swayed for hours . . .

13 the gauntlet of uniformed men so intent
14 on finding cause to turn us away. And now

15 again, we wait. We watch. Our American children
16 press against us with their small backs.

17 Which gives us pause. For the sake of the children,
18 we'll teach them to forgive the fears of others,

19 the offenses. But what we don't **anticipate**
20 is how the dust of the desert will clot our throats,

21 how much fear will conspire to keep us silent.
22 And how our children will read this silence

NOTES

23 as shame. However much we tried, we thought,
24 to **demonstrate grace**. When the buses stopped,

25 it was too dark to see the road. Or if there was a road.
26 It was night. And instead of speaking, we waited.

27 Instead of speaking, we watched.

Christine Kitano, "Gaman" from *Sky Country*. Copyright © 2017 by Christine Kitano. Reprinted with the permission of The Permissions Company, Inc., on behalf of BOA Editions Ltd., www.boaeditions.org

---

✏ **WRITE**

LITERARY ANALYSIS: Analyze how the characteristics of poetry are used to communicate the author's purpose and lend structure to "Gaman." Are the stanzas constructed similarly, or do they vary? Who is the speaker? What kinds of sound devices are used? Be sure to cite evidence from the text and specifically address stanzas, line breaks, speaker, and sound devices in your analysis.

Please note that excerpts and passages in the StudySync® library and this workbook are intended as touchstones to generate interest in an author's work. The excerpts and passages do not substitute for the reading of entire texts, and StudySync® strongly recommends that students seek out and purchase the whole literary or informational work in order to experience it as the author intended. Links to online resellers are available in our digital library. In addition, complete works may be ordered through an authorized reseller by filling out and returning to StudySync® the order form enclosed in this workbook.

Reading & Writing Companion

89

Demeter's Prayer to Hades

POETRY
Rita Dove
1995

Introduction

Rita Dove (b. 1952) is an American poet, the second African American ever to receive the Pulitzer Prize for Poetry and a former poet laureate to the Library of Congress. Her poem "Demeter's Prayer to Hades" is from Dove's collection of poems, *Mother Love*. The collection is an exploration of the mother-daughter relationship set in Dove's retelling of the Greek myth of Demeter and Persephone. Demeter, the Greek goddess of agriculture, mourns the loss of her daughter, Persephone, who was kidnapped by Hades, the Greek god of the Underworld. In this poem, imagined as a prayer from Demeter to Hades, Demeter expresses her feelings towards Hades and warns him of the consequences of his actions.

"Believe in yourself, go ahead / — see where it gets you."

1   This alone is what I wish for you: knowledge.
2   To **understand** each desire has an edge,
3   to know we are responsible for the lives
4   we change. No **faith** comes without cost,
5   no one believes without dying.
6   Now for the first time
7   I see clearly the trail you planted,
8   what ground opened to waste,
9   though you dreamed a wealth
10   of flowers.

11   There are no curses — only mirrors
12   held up to the souls of gods and **mortals**.
13   And so I give up this fate, too.
14   Believe in yourself,
15   go ahead — see where it gets you.

Persephone Returns, by Leighton, Frederic, 1891 .

From *Collected Poems 1974-2004*, by Rita Dove (W.W. Norton, 2016). Reprinted by permission of the author.

Skill:
Poetic Elements and Structure

This poem does not have a regular rhyme scheme, but the poet does rhyme the first two lines which draws attention to the message. She also uses anaphora in lines 2–3 to emphasize Demeter's message in the opening of the poem.

DEMETER'S
PRAYER
TO HADES

First Read

Read "Demeter's Prayer to Hades." After you read, complete the Think Questions below.

☁ THINK QUESTIONS

1. What is the speaker's tone in the first five lines of the first stanza? Use evidence from the poem to explain your answer.

2. What do you think the speaker means when she says, "There are no curses—only mirrors / held up to the souls of gods and mortals"? Use evidence from the text to support your answer.

3. What can the reader infer about the relationship between the "I" and the "You" in this poem? Use evidence from the text to support your answer.

4. What is the meaning of the word **faith** as it is used in the text? Write your best definition here, along with a brief explanation of how you arrived at its meaning.

5. Use context clues to determine the meaning of the word **mortals** as it is used in "Demeter's Prayer to Hades." Write your definition of *mortals* here, along with those words or phrases from the text that informed your definition. Check a dictionary to verify your understanding.

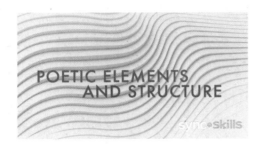

Skill:
Poetic Elements and Structure

Use the Checklist to analyze Poetic Elements and Structure in "Demeter's Prayer to Hades." Refer to the sample student annotations about Poetic Elements and Structure in the text.

••• CHECKLIST FOR POETIC ELEMENTS AND STRUCTURE

In order to identify a poet's choices concerning how to structure specific parts of a poem, and note the following:

✓ the forms and overall structure of the poem

✓ the rhyme, rhythm, and meter and the sound or feeling they create

✓ use of devices such as anaphora (repetition of a word at the beginning of succeeding lines or clauses), assonance (repetition of a sound, usually a vowel, in nearby stressed syllables), or alliteration (repetition of a sound at the beginning of nearby words)

✓ lines and stanzas in the poem that suggest its meanings and aesthetic impact

✓ how the poet began or ended the poem

✓ if the poet provided a comedic or tragic resolution

To analyze how an author's choices concerning how to structure specific parts of a text contribute to its overall structure and meaning as well as its aesthetic impact, consider the following questions:

✓ How does the poet structure the poem itself and its specific parts?

✓ How do the poet's choices contribute to the poem's overall structure and meaning as well as to its aesthetic impact?

✓ How do individual elements contribute to the sense of the poem and to its message?

Please note that excerpts and passages in the StudySync® library and this workbook are intended as touchstones to generate interest in an author's work. The excerpts and passages do not substitute for the reading of entire texts, and StudySync® strongly recommends that students seek out and purchase the whole literary or informational work in order to experience it as the author intended. Links to online resellers are available in our digital library. In addition, complete works may be ordered through an authorized reseller by filling out and returning to StudySync® the order form enclosed in this workbook.

Reading & Writing Companion 93

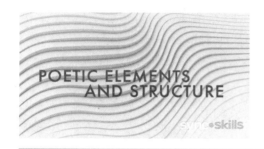

Skill: Poetic Elements and Structure

Reread lines 11–15 of "Demeter's Prayer to Hades." Then, using the Checklist on the previous page, answer the multiple-choice questions below.

↻ YOUR TURN

1. Lines 11 and 12 contain an example of —

   ○ A. anaphora

   ○ B. end rhyme

   ○ C. alliteration

   ○ D. metaphor

2. Based on lines 13–15, the speaker's perspective, or view, is that—

   ○ A. Hades must look in the mirror to understand what it is like to be mortal.

   ○ B. if Hades continues to be selfish, he will learn it leads him nowhere.

   ○ C. Hades must look in the mirror to understand what he should do in the future.

   ○ D. if Hades has faith in himself, his fate will be to one day rule the gods.

DEMETER'S
PRAYER
TO HADES

Close Read

Reread "Demeter's Prayer to Hades." As you reread, complete the Skills Focus questions below. Then use your answers and annotations from the questions to help you complete the Write activity.

◎ SKILLS FOCUS

1. Recall lines 3–4 of "Gaman," ". . . So we waited. / We watched. We thought of back home." Compare the sound devices used in these lines with those used in lines 1–4 of "Demeter's Prayer to Hades."

2. In "Gaman," some lines do not have end punctuation and may divide basic parts of a clause such as subjects and objects or modifiers and the word(s) they modify. Analyze how line breaks are used in "Demeter's Prayer to Hades," and then justify the type of use in each poem.

3. The speaker reveals a realization near the end of "Gaman" that begins with the words "But what we don't anticipate . . ." Where does Demeter reveal a new self-knowledge in "Demeter's Prayer to Hades"? Compare and contrast the realizations,

considering the impact each has on the speaker's understanding.

4. The speaker frequently refers to the darkness and the "road" in "Gaman." Locate the passage in "Demeter's Prayer to Hades" that discusses mirrors. Then analyze the context in each poem to determine the meaning of the imagery and how it relates to a theme concerning self-knowledge.

5. Explain how justice for the innocent is applied in "Gaman" and "Demeter's Prayer to Hades." Identify the type of application in each poem and the reason for its use. Cite textual evidence to support your response.

✎ WRITE

LITERARY ANALYSIS: "Demeter's Prayer to Hades" and "Gaman" both implicitly address the subject of self-knowledge and self-reflection. Analyze how each text addresses this topic. What is each author's message about self-knowledge or self-reflection? How do the poetic elements and structure of each poem help shape the author's message? How does the figurative and descriptive language in each poem help reveal the message? Are the messages in the two texts similar or different? How so? Cite evidence from the text in your analysis.

Please note that excerpts and passages in the StudySync® library and this workbook are intended as touchstones to generate interest in an author's work. The excerpts and passages do not substitute for the reading of entire texts, and StudySync® strongly recommends that students seek out and purchase the whole literary or informational work in order to experience it as the author intended. Links to online resellers are available in our digital library. In addition, complete works may be ordered through an authorized reseller by filling out and returning to StudySync® the order form enclosed in this workbook.

Reading & Writing
Companion

95

The Color of an Awkward Conversation

INFORMTIONAL TEXT
Chimamanda Ngozi Adichie
2008

Introduction

A bestselling author and winner of the National Book Critics Circle Award for her novel *Americanah*, Chimamanda Ngozi Adichie (b. 1977) has been described by *The New Yorker* as "a keen observer of American attitudes about race." The Nigerian native pursues her unique, humorous perspective on race in America in this essay.

"Still, what is most striking to me are the strange ways in which blackness is talked about."

1   I was annoyed the first time an African American man called me "sister." It was in a Brooklyn store, and I had recently arrived from Nigeria, a country where, thanks to the mosquitoes that kept British colonizers from settling, my skin color did not determine my identity, did not limit my dreams or my confidence. And so, although I grew up reading books about the **baffling** places where black people were treated badly for being black, race remained an exotic abstraction: It was Kunta Kinte.[1]

2   Until that day in Brooklyn. To be called "sister" was to be black, and blackness was the very bottom of America's pecking order. I did not want to be black.

3   In college I babysat for a Jewish family, and once I went to pick up first-grader Stephen from his play date's home. The lovely house had an American flag hanging from a colonnade. The mother of Stephen's play date greeted me warmly. Stephen hugged me and went to look for his shoes. His play date ran down the stairs and stopped halfway. "She's black," he said to his mother and stared silently at me before going back upstairs. I laughed stupidly, perhaps to deflate the tension, but I was angry.

4   I was angry that this child did not merely think that black was different but had been taught that black was not a good thing. I was angry that his behavior left Stephen bewildered, and for a long time I half-expected something **similar** to happen in other homes that displayed American flags.

5   "That kid's mother is so ignorant," one friend said. "Ignorant" suggested that an **affluent**, educated American living in a Philadelphia suburb in 1999 did not realize that black people are human beings. "It was just a kid being a kid. It wasn't racist," another said. "Racist" suggested it was no big deal, since neither the child nor his mother had burned a cross in my yard. I called the first friend a Diminisher and the second a Denier and came to discover that both represented how mainstream America talks about blackness.

---

1. **Kunta Kinte**   protagonist of Alex Haley's 1976 novel *Roots: The Saga of an American Family*, Kunta Kinte is captured and transported from Africa into slavery in the American colonies

6   Diminishers have a subtle intellectual superiority and depend on the word "ignorant." They believe that black people still encounter unpleasantness related to blackness but in **benign** forms and from unhappy people or crazy people or people with good intentions that are bungled in execution. Diminishers think that people can be "ignorant" but not "racist" because these people have black friends, supported the civil rights movements or had abolitionist forebears.

7   Deniers believe that black people stopped encountering unpleasantness related to their blackness when Martin Luther King Jr. died. They are "colorblind" and use expressions like "white, black or purple, we're all the same" — as though race were a biological rather than a social identity. Incidents that black people attribute to blackness are really about other factors, such as having too many children or driving too fast, but if deniers are compelled to accept that an incident was indeed about blackness, they launch into stories of Irish or Native American oppression, as though to deny the legitimacy of one story by generalizing about others. Deniers use "racist" as one would use "dinosaur," to refer to a phenomenon that no longer exists.

8   Although the way that blackness **manifests** itself in America has changed since 1965, the way that it is talked about has not. I have a great and complicated affection for this country — America is like my distant uncle who does not always remember my name but occasionally gives me pocket money — and what I admire most is its ability to create enduring myths. The myth of blackness is this: "Once upon a time, black towns were destroyed, black Americans were massacred and barred from voting, etc. All this happened because of racists. Today, these things no longer happen, and therefore racists no longer exist."

9   The word "racist" should be banned. It is like a sweater wrung completely out of shape; it has lost its usefulness. It makes honest debate impossible, whether about small realities such as little boys who won't say hello to black babysitters or large realities such as who is more likely to get the death penalty. In place of "racist," descriptive, albeit unwieldy, expressions might be used, such as "incidents that negatively affect black people, which, although possibly complicated by class and other factors, would not have occurred if the affected people were not black." Perhaps qualifiers would be added: "These incidents do not implicate all non-black people."

10   There are many stories like mine of Africans discovering blackness in America; of people who are consequently amused, resentful or puzzled by Americans being afraid of them or assuming they play sports or reacting to their intelligence with surprise. Still, what is most striking to me are the strange ways in which blackness is talked about. Ten years after first being called a "sister," I think of Don Cheadle as a talented brother, but I have never stopped

being aware of the relative privilege of having had those West African mosquitoes.

✎ WRITE

PERSONAL ESSAY: Chimamanda Ngozi Adichie has lived in both Nigeria and the United States and has continued to split her time between both places, which gives her a unique vantage point from which to write about race. Choose a topic on which you have a unique vantage point, and write a personal essay that describes the topic and how you view it. Why is your perspective unique? How might your experience help others look at the topic in a different light?

Extended
Oral
Project and
Grammar

EXTENDED
ORAL
PROJECT

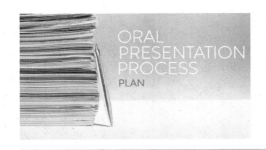

Oral Presentation Process: Plan

PLAN	DRAFT	REVISE	EDIT AND PRESENT

Members of a society are connected in many ways. Consequently, the actions of one person may, with or without intention, harm someone else. When we feel we have been wronged, we often have the right to pursue a fairer outcome, though the path to justice is rarely an easy one.

WRITING PROMPT

How can we seek justice?

"American Horse" explores justice and injustice within the family, whereas "The Color of an Awkward Conversation" and the Civil Rights Act of 1964 explore themes of justice on a national level. In each of these texts, individuals and groups advocate or yearn for a more just world. Think of a change, whether in your school or society, that you believe would result in a more just world. Then, craft a thesis to argue why this change should be made, how it should be implemented, and why it would be beneficial. Be sure to include specific evidence from the texts or outside research to support your argument. Then, consider how you might include visual aids to enhance your audience's comprehension or engagement. Additionally, use rhetorical devices in your presentation in order to persuade your audience. In order to prepare for your presentation, consider how best to meet the needs of the audience, purpose, and occasion by employing the following:

- a logical structure, including smooth transitions

- accurate evidence, well-chosen details, and rhetorical devices

- speaking techniques such as eye contact, an appropriate speaking rate and volume, enunciation, pauses for effect, purposeful gestures, and a confident and relaxed posture

- visual aids that support the information presented, including citations and a works cited list for any information obtained from outside sources

Please note that excerpts and passages in the StudySync® library and this workbook are intended as touchstones to generate interest in an author's work. The excerpts and passages do not substitute for the reading of entire texts, and StudySync® strongly recommends that students seek out and purchase the whole literary or informational work in order to experience it as the author intended. Links to online resellers are available in our digital library. In addition, complete works may be ordered through an authorized reseller by filling out and returning to StudySync® the order form enclosed in this workbook.

Reading & Writing Companion   **101**

Introduction to Oral Presentation

Compelling oral presentations use both effective speaking techniques and engaging writing to express ideas or opinions. Oral presentations can have a variety of purposes, including persuasion. The characteristics of an effective argumentative oral presentation include:

- a logical structure, including smooth transitions

- accurate evidence, well-chosen details, and rhetorical devices

- speaking techniques such as eye contact, an appropriate speaking rate and volume, enunciation, pauses for effect, purposeful gestures, and a confident and relaxed posture

- visual aids that support the information presented, including citations and a works cited list for any information obtained from outside sources

These characteristics can be organized into four major categories: context, structure, style & language, and elements of effective communication. As you continue with this Extended Oral Project, you'll receive more detailed instruction and practice in crafting each of the characteristics of argumentative writing and speaking to create your own oral presentation.

Before you get started on your own argumentative oral presentation, read this oral presentation that one student, Susie, wrote in response to the writing prompt. As you read the Model, highlight and annotate the features of oral presentation writing that Susie included in her presentation.

☰ STUDENT MODEL

NOTES

A Girl's Right to Learn

By Susie Anthony

Introduction

On mornings when frost covers our windows, the hot sun begs us outside, or we're exhausted from a restless night, going to school is the last thing we want to do. It's easy to take school for granted when its doors are wide open to us.

Introduction continued

But for one out of every five children globally, life is different. One-hundred thirty million girls worldwide are not in school ("Girls' education"). Imagine if you never had the choice to step foot into a classroom. Where would you be today? What kind of opportunities and future could you look forward to?

1 OUT OF EVERY 5 CHILDREN WORLDWIDE DOES NOT ATTEND SCHOOL.
ONE-HUNDRED THIRTY MILLION GIRLS WORLDWIDE ARE NOT IN SCHOOL.

"Girls' education," Malala Fund

NOTES

Claim

Ensuring that all citizens of the world can fully exercise their human right to an education should matter to everyone. Access to school for girls and women is particularly crucial because they have been disproportionately affected by inequalities in education.

- Educating women provides a wider range of employment options and enables women of all ages to lead healthier and more prosperous lives.

- In order to enact change, it is key to understand how gender stereotypes negatively affect women's access to education. The Right to Education Initiative emphasizes the status of education as a "multiplier right," meaning that ensuring a woman's right to education dramatically increases her chances of improving her socioeconomic status by safeguarding "key rights, such as those related to work, property, political participation, access to justice, freedom from violence and health."

Education Makes a Difference

- Educating women enables women of all ages to lead healthier and more prosperous lives.
- Education dramatically increases a woman's chances of improving her socioeconomic status by safeguarding her "key rights."

NOTES

Evidence and Analysis #1

Historical gender disparities in education have had a dramatic impact on women. For instance, over two-thirds of the nearly 800 million illiterate people in the world are women ("Facts & Figures").

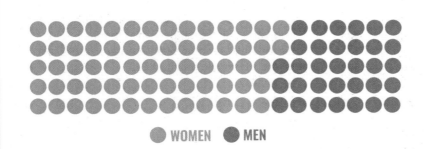

● WOMEN ● MEN

GLOBAL ILLITERACY RATES BY GENDER

"Facts & Figures," UN Women

Evidence and Analysis #2

Women's access to quality education in locations across the globe is blocked by a variety of factors.

- Many girls are pressured into the labor market at a young age in order to support their families. Instead of getting an education and learning the skills they need for professional employment, girls work in low-skilled jobs for low wages, which is detrimental to their health and development.

- A lack of education funding in some countries means families are required to pay for any education their child receives. For many families, especially those living in poor countries, the fees are prohibitive.

- Some schools even lack basic resources. Many students have to make long journeys to and from school (UNICEF).

NOTES

Education Is Withheld for a Variety of Reasons

- Many girls are pressured into the labor market at a young age in order to support their families.
- Lack of education funding in some countries means families are required to pay for any education that their child receives.
- Some schools lack even basic resources and require students to make long journeys to and from school (UNICEF).

Evidence and Analysis #3

Educating women is beneficial on an individual and global scale because it is a multiplier right.

- Women with a secondary school education earn more money and are better able to support themselves and their families.

- The World Bank also found that not educating women "costs countries between $15 trillion and $30 trillion in lost lifetime productivity and earnings."

- Increased access to education means more women in the workforce and more people contributing to the world's economy.

- Investing in education for women, therefore, initiates a chain reaction that positively benefits women *and* society as a whole.

Educating Women Helps Everyone

- Women earn more money and are able to support themselves.
- Lack of education "costs countries between $15 trillion and $30 trillion in lost lifetime productivity and earnings" (The World Bank).
- More women in the workforce means more people contributing to the world's economy.

Evidence and Analysis #4

Organizations like the Malala Fund are working to increase girls' access to education.

- This non-profit organization supports women's education and gives young girls a platform to share their experiences.

Evidence and Analysis #5

The successful achievement of providing worldwide access to K–12 education for girls requires people to evaluate their own stereotypes about gender.

- In order to enact change, it is key to understand how gender stereotypes negatively affect women's access to education. Organizations like the Right to Education Initiative address gender stereotypes as a key factor in educational reform. They do not seek to change people's beliefs. Rather, they aim to point out that "gender stereotyping is considered *wrongful* when it results in a violation or violations of human rights and fundamental freedoms" ("Women and girls").

NOTES

Gender Stereotypes

- Education for girls requires people to evaluate their own stereotypes about gender.
- Gender stereotypes negatively affect women's access to education.

Counterargument

You might be familiar with the stereotype that women's cognitive abilities are better suited for the arts and humanities. Such gender stereotypes discourage girls and women from pursuing STEM-related degrees or careers, producing inequality in education and employment.

- For example, gender stereotypes produce inequality in employment. Women represent 47% of the workforce, but only 12% of engineers ("Women in Computer Science"). A disproportionate percentage of men reap the monetary benefits of careers in engineering. Additionally, gender stereotypes lead to unequal political participation and representation. Consequently, women have limited access to or are barred from positions of power, which they could use to advocate for women's rights.

Gender Stereotypes

- A disproportionate percentage of men reap the monetary benefits of careers in engineering.
- Women have limited access to or are barred from positions of power, which they can use to advocate for women's rights.

Counterargument continued

The gender stereotype of domesticity is considered harmful when girls are forced to marry and bear children before the age of 18.

- According to the Global Partnership for Education, "Child marriage leads girls to have children earlier and more children over their lifetime. This in turn reduces the ability of households to meet their basic needs, and thereby contributes to poverty" (Wodon).

- Jessica Chastain sums up the issues with this practice in an interview with ABC (watch the interview in the Plan lesson on the StudySync site).

- The knowledge women gain in school prepares them to make better healthcare decisions for themselves and their families. Furthermore, non-adolescent mothers and their children have lower rates of health complications and mortality ("Missed Opportunities").

Conclusion

The ways in which girls and women worldwide are subjected to discrimination cannot be encapsulated by a single narrative. If we are to create justice, we must keep in mind that women all over the world face inequality in different ways. This may seem like a tall order, but the first step is to pay attention to experiences outside of our own. Denying a woman's right to equal education is also a denial of her rights to freedom and representation.

Thank you for your attention! I hope you've gained a better understanding of the benefits of providing education to girls worldwide.

"When girls are educated, their countries become stronger and are more prosperous."

- Michelle Obama, FLOTUS Travel Journal: An Example to Follow

Conclusion continued

Elevating the status of women worldwide through equal access to education will improve the lives of deserving individuals and help cultivate future generations of enlightened leaders.

Works Cited

"About Us." Girls Who Code. Girls Who Code, girlswhocode.com/about-us/?nabe=6554069360181248:0.

Cook, Rebecca J., and Simone Cusack. Gender Stereotyping: Transnational Legal Perspectives. University of Pennsylvania Press, 2010.

"The Current State of Women in Computer Science." ComputerScience.Org, ComputerScience.Org, www.computerscience.org/resources/women-in-computer-science/.

"Facts & Figures." UN Women, www.unwomen.org/en/news/in-focus/commission-on-the-status-of-women-2012/facts-and-figures.

"Girls' education." Malala Fund, Malala Fund, www.malala.org/girls-education.

Global Partnership for Education, Global Partnership for Education, 29 June 2017, www.globalpartnership.org/blog/child-marriage-and-education-impacts-costs-and-benefit.

"Jessica Chastain talks about gender inequality around the globe." NBC News Archives Express, featuring Jessica Chastain, NBCUniversal Media, LLC. 2 June 2013, www.nbcnewsarchivesxpress.com/contentdetails/195331.

"Missed Opportunities: The High Cost of Not Educating Girls." The World Bank, World Bank Group, 11 July 2018, www.worldbank.org/en/topic/education/publication/missed-opportunities-the-high-cost-of-not-educating-girls.

Obama, Michelle. "FLOTUS Travel Journal: An Example to Follow." The White House Archives, National Archives and Records Administration, 27 June 2013, obamawhitehouse.archives.gov/blog/2013/06/27/flotus-travel-journal-example-follow.

"One in every five children, adolescents, and youth is out of school worldwide." UNESCO, UNESCO, en.unesco.org/news/one-every-five-children-adolescents-and-youth-out-school-worldwide.

"Supplies and Logistics: Education." UNICEF, UNICEF, www.unicef.org/supply/index_education.html.

Wodon, Quentin. "Child marriage and education: impacts, costs, and benefits."

"Women and girls." Right to Education, Right to Education Initiative, www.right-to-education.org/girlswomen.

Works Cited

"About Us." *Girls Who Code*, Girls Who Code, girlswhocode.com/about-us/?nabe=6554069360181248:0.

Cook, Rebecca J., and Simone Cusack. *Gender Stereotyping: Transnational Legal Perspectives*. University of Pennsylvania Press, 2010.

"The Current State of Women in Computer Science." *ComputerScience. Org*, ComputerScience.Org, www.computerscience.org/resources/women-in-computer-science/.

"Facts & Figures." *UN Women*, UN Women, www.unwomen.org/en/news/in-focus/commission-on-the-status-of-women-2012/facts-and-figures.

"Girls' education." *Malala Fund*, Malala Fund, www.malala.org/girls-education.

"Jessica Chastain talks about gender inequality around the globe." *NBC News Archives Express*, featuring Jessica Chastain, NBCUniversal Media, LLC, 2 June 2013, https://www.nbcnewsarchivesxpress.com/contentdetails/195331.

"Missed Opportunities: The High Cost of Not Educating Girls." *The World Bank*, World Bank Group, 11 July 2018, www.worldbank.org/en/topic/education/publication/missed-opportunities-the-high-cost-of-not-educating-girls.

Obama, Michelle. "FLOTUS Travel Journal: An Example to Follow." *The White House Archives*, National Archives and Records Administration, 27 June 2013, obamawhitehouse.archives.gov/blog/2013/06/27/flotus-travel-journal-example-follow.

"One in every five children, adolescents, and youth is out of school worldwide." *UNESCO*, UNESCO, 28 Feb. 2018, en.unesco.org/news/one-every-five-children-adolescents-and-youth-out-school-worldwide.

Please note that excerpts and passages in the StudySync® library and this workbook are intended as touchstones to generate interest in an author's work. The excerpts and passages do not substitute for the reading of entire texts, and StudySync® strongly recommends that students seek out and purchase the whole literary or informational work in order to experience it as the author intended. Links to online resellers are available in our digital library. In addition, complete works may be ordered through an authorized reseller by filling out and returning to StudySync® the order form enclosed in this workbook.

Reading & Writing Companion

111

"Supplies and Logistics: Education." *UNICEF*, UNICEF, 23 June 2016, www.unicef.org/supply/index_education.html.

Wodon, Quentin. "Child marriage and education: impacts, costs, and benefits." *Global Partnership for Education*, Global Partnership for Education, 29 June 2017, www.globalpartnership.org/blog/child-marriage-and-education-impacts-costs-and-benefits.

"Women and girls." *Right to Education*, Right to Education Initiative, www.right-to-education.org/girlswomen.

✏ WRITE

When you write, it is important to consider your audience and purpose so you can write appropriately for them. Your purpose is implied in the writing prompt. Reread the prompt to determine your purpose for writing.

To begin, review the questions below and then select a strategy, such as brainstorming, journaling, reading, or discussing, to generate ideas.

- **Purpose:** What will be the focus of your presentation, and what important ideas do you want to convey?

- **Audience:** Who is your audience, and what message do you want to express to your audience?

- **Thesis:** What claim will you argue about a change that will create a more just world?

- **Evidence:** What facts, evidence, and details might you include? Which texts will help you support your ideas? What other research might you need to do? What anecdotes from your personal life or what background knowledge is relevant to the topic of your presentation?

- **Organization:** How can you organize your presentation so that it is clear and easy to follow?

- **Clear Communication:** How will you make sure that your audience can hear and understand what you are saying?

- **Gestures and Visual Aids:** What illustrations or other visual aids could you use during your presentation? What effect will they have on your audience? What physical gestures and body language will help you communicate your ideas?

Response Instructions

Use the questions in the bulleted list and the ideas you generated to write a one-paragraph summary. Your summary should describe what you will discuss in your oral presentation.

Don't worry about including all of the details now; focus only on the most essential and important elements. You will refer to this short summary as you continue through the steps of the writing process.

Please note that excerpts and passages in the StudySync® library and this workbook are intended as touchstones to generate interest in an author's work. The excerpts and passages do not substitute for the reading of entire texts, and StudySync® strongly recommends that students seek out and purchase the whole literary or informational work in order to experience it as the author intended. Links to online resellers are available in our digital library. In addition, complete works may be ordered through an authorized reseller by filling out and returning to StudySync® the order form enclosed in this workbook.

Reading & Writing Companion 113

Skill: Organizing an Oral Presentation

••• CHECKLIST FOR ORGANIZING AN ORAL PRESENTATION

In order to present information, findings, and supporting evidence conveying a clear and distinct perspective, do the following:

- choose a style for your oral presentation, either formal or informal
- determine whether the development and organization of your presentation, as well as its substance and style, are appropriate for your purpose, audience, and task
- determine whether your presentation conveys a clear and distinct perspective so that listeners can follow your line of reasoning
- make sure you address alternative perspectives that oppose your own in your presentation
- make strategic, or deliberate, use of digital media, such as textual, graphical, audio, visual, and interactive elements, to add interest and enhance your audience's understanding of the findings, reasoning, and evidence in your presentation

To present information, findings, and supporting evidence conveying a clear and distinct perspective, consider the following questions:

- Did I make sure that the information in my presentation conveys a clear and distinct perspective, so that listeners can follow my line of reasoning?
- Have I presented opposing or alternative viewpoints in my presentation?
- Did I make sure that the information in my presentation follows a logical order, so my listeners can follow my line of reasoning?
- Are the organization, development, substance, and style appropriate for my purpose and audience?
- Have I made strategic use of media to add interest and enhance my audience's understanding of my presentation?

⟳ YOUR TURN

Read the sentences below. Then, complete the chart on the next page by determining where each sentence belongs in the outline. Write the corresponding letter for each sentence in the appropriate row.

	Sentences
A	I will provide examples of regions in need of resilient farming practices like Central America's Dry Corridor where agricultural production is affected by years of drought. I will also discuss successful initiatives such as how the Food and Agriculture Organization installed fisheries and coconut-based farming systems in the Philippines after Typhoon Haiyan.
B	I can use words like *next*, *since*, and *additionally* to improve the logical progression of my ideas.
C	Many people in the world rely on farming, livestock, fishing, etc., to feed their families and make a living. Every year, people become hungry or food insecure after natural disasters eliminate their source of food or income. People need to be educated about sustainable farming practices to eliminate hunger and reduce the risk of a world food crisis. We need to support farmers and build resilience against the challenges of climate change, malnutrition, and poverty.
D	In the end, I will reiterate the importance of taking action now to prevent a world food crisis. I will rephrase my thesis and summarize my main points.
E	I can include photos of locations devastated by violent weather and drought.
F	I want to convince people why it is important to collaborate and protect communities that depend heavily on farming from devastation due to natural disasters.
G	Some people might think that it is more important to invest in more secure food sources like genetically modified crops. I will explain the shortcomings of such an approach.

Purpose	
Introduction / Thesis Statement	
Body / Evidence	
Alternative/Opposing Viewpoints	
Visual Aids and Digital Media	
Logical Progression	
Conclusion / Rephrasing of Thesis	

✏ WRITE

Use the questions in the checklist to outline your formal oral presentation. Be sure to include a clear thesis and a logical progression of valid evidence from reliable sources.

Skill:
Evaluating Sources

••• CHECKLIST FOR EVALUATING SOURCES

First, reread the sources you gathered and identify the following:

- where information seems inaccurate, biased, or outdated
- where information strongly relates to your task, purpose, and audience
- where information helps you make an informed decision or solve a problem

In order to conduct advanced searches to gather relevant, credible, and accurate print and digital sources, use the following questions as a guide:

- Is the material published by a well-established source or expert author?
- Is the source material written by a recognized expert on the topic or a well-respected author or organization?
- Is the material up-to-date or based on the most current information?
- Is the source based on factual information that can be verified by another source?
- Are there discrepancies between the information presented in different sources?
- Is the source material objective and unbiased?
- Does the source contain omissions of important information that supports other viewpoints?
- Does the source contain faulty reasoning?

In order to refine your search process, consider the following questions:

- Are there specific terms or phrases that I can use to adjust my search?
- Can I use *and, or,* or *not* to expand or limit my search?
- Can I use quotation marks to search for exact phrases?

Please note that excerpts and passages in the StudySync® library and this workbook are intended as touchstones to generate interest in an author's work. The excerpts and passages do not substitute for the reading of entire texts, and StudySync® strongly recommends that students seek out and purchase the whole literary or informational work in order to experience it as the author intended. Links to online resellers are available in our digital library. In addition, complete works may be ordered through an authorized reseller by filling out and returning to StudySync® the order form enclosed in this workbook.

Reading & Writing
Companion

117

⟳ YOUR TURN

Read the factors below. Then, complete the chart by sorting the factors into two categories: those that are credible and reliable and those that are not. Write the corresponding letter for each factor in the appropriate column.

Factors	
A	The author holds an advanced degree in a subject related to your topic of research.
B	The text is objective and includes perspectives that are properly cited.
C	The article states only the author's personal opinions.
D	The text makes uncited claims to persuade readers.
E	The article includes clear arguments that are supported by factual information.
F	The article is not peer reviewed or published anywhere of note.

Credible and Reliable	Not Credible or Reliable

YOUR TURN

Complete the chart below by filling in the title and author of a source for your presentation and answering the questions about it.

Questions	Answers
Source Title and Author:	
Reliability: Has the source material been published in a well-established book or periodical or on a well-established website? Is the source material up-to-date or based on the most current information?	
Accuracy: Is the source based on factual information that can be verified by another source?	
Credibility: Is the source material written by a recognized expert on the topic? Is the source material published by a well-respected author or organization?	
Bias: Is the source material objective and unbiased?	
Omission: Does the source contain omissions of important information that supports other viewpoints?	
Faulty Reasoning: Does the source contain faulty reasoning?	
Should I use this source in my presentation?	

Skill: Considering Audience and Purpose

••• CHECKLIST FOR CONSIDERING AUDIENCE AND PURPOSE

In order to present information, findings, and supporting evidence so that listeners can follow the line of reasoning and to ensure that the organization, development, substance, and style of your presentation are appropriate for the purpose, audience, and task, note the following:

- when writing your presentation, convey and maintain a clear and distinct perspective or viewpoint
- check the development and organization of the information in your presentation to see that they are appropriate for your purpose, audience, and task
- determine whether the substance, or basis of your presentation, is also appropriate for your purpose, audience, and task
- remember to adapt your presentation to your task, and if it is appropriate, use formal English and not language you would use in ordinary conversation

To better understand how to present information, findings, and supporting evidence so that listeners can follow the line of reasoning and to ensure that the organization, development, substance, and style of your presentation are appropriate for the purpose, audience, and task, consider the following questions:

- Have I organized the information in my presentation so that my perspective is clear?
- Have I developed and organized the information so that it is appropriate for my purpose, audience, and task?
- Are the substance and style suitable?

⟳ YOUR TURN

Read each statement below. Then, complete the chart by identifying whether the statements are appropriate for a formal presentation. Write the corresponding letter for each statement in the appropriate column.

	Statements
A	She was definitely the best NCAA soccer player that year.
B	Knowing basic first aid could help save lives.
C	According to its spokesperson, the labor union demands fair compensation for its members' work.
D	Some people seem to think that drinking green tea is the key to health, but I'm not sure if I can get on board with that.
E	I can't believe you don't know about Frank Lloyd Wright.
F	The majority of teachers reported an increase in student participation following the implementation of electronic tablets in the classroom.

Appropriate	Inappropriate

Please note that excerpts and passages in the StudySync® library and this workbook are intended as touchstones to generate interest in an author's work. The excerpts and passages do not substitute for the reading of entire texts, and StudySync® strongly recommends that students seek out and purchase the whole literary or informational work in order to experience it as the author intended. Links to online resellers are available in our digital library. In addition, complete works may be ordered through an authorized reseller by filling out and returning to StudySync® the order form enclosed in this workbook.

Reading & Writing Companion

121

YOUR TURN

Complete the chart by answering each question about your presentation.

Question	My Response
What is my purpose, and who is my audience?	
Do I plan to use formal or informal language?	
What sort of tone, or attitude, do I want to convey?	
How would I describe the voice I would like to use in my presentation?	
How will I use vocabulary and language to create that particular voice?	

Skill:
Persuasive Techniques

••• CHECKLIST FOR PERSUASIVE TECHNIQUES

In order to draft argumentative oral presentations, use the following steps:

1. First, consider your audience and purpose by asking:

   • Who is my primary audience? What is my audience's primary motivation?

   • What is my purpose? What do I hope to achieve?

2. Next, think about the following persuasive techniques and the ways you might use one or more:

   • Appeals to Logic

     > What facts or statistics will persuade my audience to agree with my argument?

     > What is the most effective way to present factual information to persuade my audience that my argument is logically sound and reasonable?

   • Appeals to Emotion

     > What emotions do I want my audience to feel about my topic?

     > What words or phrases should I include to bring about those feelings in my audience?

   • Appeals to Ethics

     > Which experts could I use to establish the credibility of my claims?

     > What words or phrases should I include to remind my audience of our shared values?

   • Rhetorical Devices

     > How can I use language in artful and persuasive ways to convince my audience?

     > What specific rhetorical devices, such as rhetorical questions, repetition, or parallelism, do I want to use to make my argument more persuasive?

   • Counterclaim

     > What is an opposing opinion that my audience might have?

     > How can I rebut that opposing opinion in a way that respects my audience and strengthens my argument?

YOUR TURN

Read the appeals below. Then, complete the chart by placing each appeal in the appropriate category. Write the corresponding letter for each appeal in the appropriate column.

	Appeals
A	Decorating your home with plants will have a positive influence on your mood.
B	The president of the local food bank has worked on issues of food security for over 25 years.
C	You should stay away from isolated tall trees during a thunderstorm because lightning tends to strike the taller objects in an area.
D	Having worked as a counselor, teacher, and advocate for youth for many years, the new Youth Services director had a reputation for fairness, being a good listener, and taking the concerns of young people seriously.
E	There is no greater satisfaction than watching your child succeed.
F	You can save money on groceries by using coupons.

Appeal to Logic	Appeal to Emotion	Appeal to Ethics

WRITE

Use the questions in the checklist to brainstorm persuasive techniques you will use in your presentation. When you have finished brainstorming, write notes explaining how you will use the techniques.

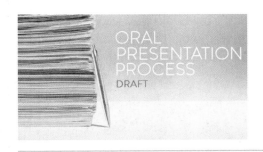

Oral Presentation Process: Draft

| PLAN | DRAFT | REVISE | EDIT AND PRESENT |

You have already made progress toward writing your argumentative oral presentation. Now it is time to draft your argumentative oral presentation.

✎ WRITE

Use your plan and other responses in your Binder to draft your argumentative oral presentation. You may also have new ideas as you begin drafting. Feel free to explore those new ideas as you have them. You can also ask yourself these questions to ensure that your writing is focused, organized, and developed:

Draft Checklist:

- **Focused:** Is the topic of my presentation clear to my audience? Have I included only relevant information and details about my topic? Have I avoided extraneous details that might confuse or distract my audience?

- **Organized:** Is the organization of ideas and events in my presentation logical? Have I reinforced this logical structure with transitional words and phrases to help my audience follow the order of ideas?

- **Developed:** Do all of my details support my thesis about why this change would promote justice in the world? Do I have enough evidence from different sources to support my thesis?

Before you submit your draft, read it over carefully. You want to be sure that you've responded to all aspects of the prompt.

Here is Susie's argumentative oral presentation draft. As you read, notice how Susie develops her draft to be focused, organized, and developed. As she continues to revise and edit her argumentative oral presentation, she will find and improve weak spots in her writing, as well as correct any language or punctuation mistakes.

NOTES

☰ STUDENT MODEL: FIRST DRAFT

A Girl's Right to Learn

Sometimes going to school is a bummer. It's easy to take school for granted when its doors are wide open to us. But for one out of every five children globaly, life is different. One-hundred thirty million girls worldwide are not in school (Malala Fund). Imagine if you never had the choice to step foot into a classroom.

~~Enshering that all citizens of the world can fully exercise their human right to an education should matter to everyone, especially to students like you and me. Access to school for girls and women is particularly crushal when they are disproportionately affected by inequalities in education. For instance, over two thirds of the nearly 800 million illiterit people in the world are women (UN Women). Educating women provides a wider range of employment options. The Right to Education Initiative emphasizes the status of education as a "multiplier right."~~

Claim

Ensuring that all citizens of the world can fully exercise their human right to an education should matter to everyone. Access to school for girls and women is particularly crucial because they have been disproportionately affected by inequalities in education.

- Educating women provides a wider range of employment options and enables women of all ages to lead healthier and more prosperous lives.

- In order to enact change, it is key to understand how gender stereotypes negatively affect women's access to education. The Right to Education Initiative emphasizes the status of education as a "multiplier right," meaning that ensuring a woman's right to education dramatically increases her chances of improving her

Skill:
Communicating
Ideas

Susie decides to show slides highlighting her key ideas throughout her presentation. As she discusses the ideas, she'll point to them on the slides. She'll use these gestures to focus the audience's attention on the information and help keep her listeners engaged.

socioeconomic status by safeguarding "key rights, such as those related to work, property, political participation, access to justice, freedom from violence and health."

[Show slide with a bulleted list of ideas, titled "Education Makes a Difference."]

Women's access to quality education in locations across the globe is impeded or blocked by a variety of economic, geographical, and political factors. Many girls are pressured into the labor market at a young age in order to support their families. Girls work in low-skilled jobs for low wages. A lack of education funding in some countries means families are required to pay for any education their child receives. The fees are prohibitive for many families, especially those living in poor countries. There are countries that do provide free access to education. But even in such countries, budget limitations lead to a shortage of trained educators, overcrowding, and no support for students with additional learning needs. Some schools even lack basic resources such as suffishent shelter, desks, chairs, school supplies, books, and bathroom facilities (UNICEF). Many students across the world long journeys to and from school everyday. Some places have violent conflicts that make commuting to and attending school dangerous.

~~Educating women is beneficial on an individual and global scale because it is a multiplier right. Women with secondary school education earn more money. According to The World Bank in July 2018, "women with secondary school education earn almost twice as much as those with no education at all." The World Bank also found that not educating women "costs countries between $15 trillion and $30 trillion in lost lifetime and productivity and earnings." Increased access to education means more women in the workforce. Investing in education for women, therefore, has a chane reaction~~ that positively benefits women *and* ~~society as whole.~~

Evidence and Analysis #3

Educating women is beneficial on an individual and global scale because it is a multiplier right.

- Women with a secondary school education earn more money and are better able to support themselves and their families.

Skill: Engaging in Discourse

Susie's partner points out that Susie hasn't explained how educating women benefits "society as a whole." So Susie expands on the significance of her evidence, adding details that improve the coherence of this section of her presentation.

- The World Bank also found that not educating women "costs countries between $15 trillion and $30 trillion in lost lifetime productivity and earnings."

- Increased access to education means more women in the workforce and more people contributing to the world's economy.

- Investing in education for women, therefore, initiates a chain reaction that positively benefits women *and* society as a whole.

[Show slide with bullet points.]

Organizations like the Malala Fund are working to increase girls' access to education. The Malala Fund was founded by Pakistani activist and Nobel Prize laureate Malala Yousafzai and her father Ziauddin Yousafzai. The Malala Fund advocates for twelve years of free, safe, and quality education for all girls worldwide. This non-profit organization supports women's education through an international network of dedicated educational activists. The goal of the network is to give girls a secondary education so they are "more able and likely to contribute fully in their families, communities and societies, as earners, informed mothers, and agents of change" (Malala Fund). The work of the Malala Fund includes filanthropy, recruiting teachers, developing student outreach programs, and giving young girls a platform to share their experiences. Anyone can contribute on a smaller scale through donations or by speaking about this issue to raise awareness.

The goal of providing worldwide access to K–12 education for girls and women is not impeded solely by economic factors, however. The successful achievement of this goal also requires people to be less lazy when thinking about gender. *Gender Stereotyping: Transnational Legal Perspectives* says a gender stereotype is "a generalised view or preconception about attributes or characteristics that are or ought to be possessed by, or the roles that are or should be performed by women and men." It is key to understand how gender stereotypes work. Organizations like the Right to Education Initiative address gender stereotypes as a key factor in educational reform. They do not seek change people's beliefs rather they aim to point out that "gender stereotyping is considered *wrongful* when it results in a violation or violations of human rights and fundamental freedoms" ("Women and girls").

~~You might be familiar with the stereotype that women's cognitive abilities are better suited for the arts and humanities than math and sciences. Such gender stereotypes discourage girls and women from pursuing STEM-related degrees or careers, producing inequality in education and employment. Women represent 47% of the workforce, but only 12% of engineers ("Women in Computer Science"). A disproportionate percentage of men reap the monetary benefits of careers in engineering. Programs are working to close the gender gap in technology by offering learning opportunities and career pathways for female engineers. Also lead to unequal political participation and representation. Women have limited access to, or are barred from, positions of power that they could use to advocate for women's rights. This is unjust because this denies women their right to equal education, employment, and representation.~~

Counterargument

Skill:
Transitions

You might be familiar with the stereotype that women's cognitive abilities are better suited for the arts and humanities. Such gender stereotypes discourage girls and women from pursuing STEM-related degrees or careers, producing inequality in education and employment.

Susie realizes that she should clarify the connections between her sentences. She adds the transitions for example and consequently to help her audience follow the sequence of her ideas.

- For example, gender stereotypes produce inequality in employment. Women represent 47% of the workforce, but only 12% of engineers ("Women in Computer Science"). A disproportionate percentage of men reap the monetary benefits of careers in engineering. Additionally, gender stereotypes lead to unequal political participation and representation. Consequently, women have limited access to or are barred from positions of power, which they could use to advocate for women's rights.

[Show slide with bullet points.]

~~Another stereotype is the belief that a young women's education should prepare them for domestic duties as a wife and mother, rendering a formal education unnecessary. This gender stereotype considered harmful when girls are forced to marry and bear children before the age of 18. Advocating for all women's right to an education~~

**Skill:
Reasons and
Evidence**

*Susie wants to
strengthen her point
about the gender
stereotype of
domesticity. She includes
support to show why the
stereotype is harmful
and why education is
beneficial.*

**Skill:
Sources and
Citations**

*Susie provides citations
for the quotation and
paraphrased information
that she adds to this
section of her
presentation. She
includes the author's last
name in the first citation.
In the second citation,
she lists the title of the
work since the author is
not known.*

~~nessessitates enforcing laws to protect children from underaged marriages. Education creates more opportunities in life for women beyond marriage and motherhood.~~

Counterargument continued

The gender stereotype of domesticity is considered harmful when girls are forced to marry and bear children before the age of 18.

- According to the Global Partnership for Education, "Child marriage leads girls to have children earlier and more children over their lifetime. This in turn reduces the ability of households to meet their basic needs, and thereby contributes to poverty" (Wodon).

- Jessica Chastain sums up the issues with this practice in an interview with ABC. [Show video of Jessica Chastain interview.]

- The knowledge women gain in school prepares them to make better healthcare decisions for themselves and their families. Furthermore, non-adolescent mothers and their children have lower rates of health complications and mortality ("Missed Opportunities").

The ways in which girls and women worldwide are subjected to discrimination varies widely. If we are to create justice, we must keep in mind that women all over the world face inequality in different ways. This may seem like a tall order. The first step is to pay attention to experiences outside of our own. Denying a woman's right to equal education prevents her from living a healthy and fruitful life. Denying a woman's right to equal education is also a denial of her rights to freedom and representation. Therefore, we must give the girls and women of the world a voice by sharing their stories and looking for justice. Consider the words of Former First Lady Michelle Obama, "When girls are educated, their countries become stronger and more prosperous," thus elevating the status of women worldwide through equal access to education will improve the lives of deserving individuals and help cultivate future generations of enlightened leaders.

Sources

"About Us." *Girls Who Code*, girlswhocode.com/about-us/?nabe= 6554069360181248:0. Accessed 19 Dec. 2018.

Arveen. "25 Women's Education Quotes That Prove School Matters." *Live Your Dream*, 13 Sept. 2018, yourdream.liveyourdream. org/2017/06/25-education-quotes/. Accessed 19 Dec 2018.

Wodon, Quentin. "Child marriage and education: impacts, costs, and benefits." *Global Partnership for Education*, 29 June 2017, www. globalpartnership.org/blog/child-marriage-and-education-impacts-costs-and-benefits. Accessed 19 Dec 2018.

Cook, Rebecca J., and Simone Cusack. *Gender Stereotyping: Transnational Legal Perspectives*. University of Pennsylvania Press, 2010.

"The Current State of Women in Computer Science." *Computer Science*, www.computerscience.org/resources/women-in-computer-science/. Accessed 17 Dec. 2018.

"Facts & Figures." *UN Women*, www.unwomen.org/en/news/in-focus/commission-on-the-status-of-women-2012/facts-and-figures. Access 18 Dec. 2018.

"Girls' education." *Malala Fund*, www.malala.org/girls-education. Accessed 17 Dec. 2018.

"Leaving no one behind: How far on the way to universal primary and secondary education?" *United Nations. Educational, Scientific, and Cultural Organization*, 2016, en.unesco.org/gem-report/leaving-no-one-behind-how-far-way-universal-primary-and-secondary-education. Accessed 19 Dec 2018.

"Missed Opportunities: The High Cost of Not Educating Girls." *The World Bank*, www.worldbank.org/en/topic/education/publication/missed-opportunities-the-high-cost-of-not-educating-girls. Accessed 17 Dec. 2018.

"One in every five children, adolescents, and youth is out of school worldwide."*UNESCO*,en.unesco.org/news/one-every-five-children-adolescents-and-youth-out-school-worldwide. Accessed 18 Dec. 2018.

"Supplies and Logistics: Education." *UNICEF*, www.unicef.org/supply/index_education.html. Accessed 19 Dec 2018.

UNICEF Supply Division. "School Furniture Innovation Project: Field Trial Results." *UNICEF*, March 2016, www.unicef.org/supply/index_90797.html. Accessed 19 Dec 2018.

"Women and girls." *Right to Education, www.right-to-education.org/girlswomen.* Accessed 17 Dec. 2018.

Copyright © BookheadEd Learning, LLC

Skill:
Transitions

••• CHECKLIST FOR TRANSITIONS

Before you revise your current draft to include transitions, think about:

- the key ideas you discuss
- the major sections of your oral presentation
- the organizational structure of your oral presentation
- the relationships between complex ideas and concepts

Next, reread your current draft and note places in your oral presentation where:

- the organizational structure is not yet apparent
  - > For example, if you are comparing and contrasting ideas, your explanations about how these ideas are similar and different should be clearly stated
- the relationship between ideas from one paragraph to the next is unclear
  - > For example, when you describe a process in sequential order, you should clarify the order of the steps by using transitional words like *first, then, next,* and *finally*
- your ideas do not create cohesion, or a unified whole
- your transitions and/or syntax is inappropriate

Revise your draft to use appropriate and varied transitions and syntax to link the major sections of your oral presentation, create cohesion, and clarify the relationships between complex ideas and concepts, using the following questions as a guide:

- What kind of transitions should I use to make the organizational structure clear to readers?
- Are my transitions linking the major sections of my oral presentation?
- What transitions create cohesion between complex ideas and concepts?
- Are my transitions and syntax varied and appropriate?
  - > Have my transitions clarified the relationships between complex ideas and concepts?

Copyright © BookheadEd Learning, LLC

YOUR TURN

Choose the best answer to each question.

1. Below is a passage from a previous draft of Susie's oral presentation. The connection between the two sentences is unclear. What transition should Susie add to the beginning of the second sentence to make her writing more coherent and fluid?

> United States federal law requires equity in education as well as in athletics. Girls across the nation are discouraged from playing sports due to gender inequalities in their school athletic programs.

○ A. Although this may be true,

○ B. Eventually,

○ C. Particularly,

○ D. As a result,

2. Below is a passage from a previous draft of Susie's argumentative oral presentation. Susie did not use an appropriate transition to show the relationship between the paragraphs. Which of the following transitions is the best replacement for the word *unless*? Choose the transition that makes her writing more fluid and is the most appropriate for the purpose, topic, and context of her presentation, as well as her audience.

> Due to overcrowding, many students do not get the individualized attention they need to thrive in school.
>
> Unless, the National Center for Education Statistics found that a high student to teacher ratio has a negative effect on standardized testing scores.

○ A. Initially,

○ B. Although,

○ C. On the other hand,

○ D. As a matter of fact,

 WRITE

Use the questions in the checklist to revise your argumentative oral presentation so that it exhibits fluid and coherent transitions.

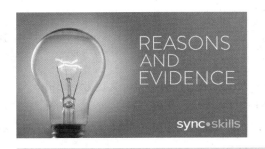

Skill:
Reasons and Evidence

••• CHECKLIST FOR REASONS AND EVIDENCE

In order to identify a speaker's point of view, reasoning, and use of evidence and rhetoric, note the following:

- the stance, or position, the speaker takes on a topic
- whether the premise, or the basis of the speech or talk, is based on logical reasoning
- whether the ideas follow one another in a way that shows clear, sound thinking
- whether the speaker employs the use of exaggeration, especially when citing facts or statistics
- the speaker's choice of words, the points he or she chooses to emphasize, and the tone, or general attitude

In order to evaluate a speaker's point of view, reasoning, and use of evidence and rhetoric, consider the following questions:

- What stance, or position, does the speaker take? Is the premise based on sound, logical reasoning? Why or why not?
- Does the speaker use facts and statistics to make a point? Are they exaggerated?
- What points does the speaker choose to emphasize?
- How does the speaker's choice of words affect his or her tone?

YOUR TURN

Read the examples of reasoning from a draft of Susie's oral presentation below. Then, complete the chart by sorting the examples into two categories: those that are logical and those that are illogical. Write the corresponding letter for each example in the appropriate column.

Examples	
A	Organizations like the Malala Fund are working to increase girls' access to education, thus providing an important service.
B	The Malala Fund is a really cool organization that will eliminate all inequalities in education.
C	These gender stereotypes discourage girls and women from pursuing STEM-related degrees or careers, producing equality in education and employment.
D	Such gender stereotypes discourage girls and women from pursuing STEM-related degrees or careers, producing inequality in education and employment.
E	All women face inequality, and we have to come up with a single solution that works for everyone to make it better.
F	If we are to create justice, we must keep in mind that women all over the world face inequality in different ways.

Logical Reasoning	Illogical Reasoning

⟳ YOUR TURN

Below are three examples of an ineffective use of evidence from a previous draft of Susie's oral presentation. In the second column, rewrite the sentences to use the evidence effectively, without exaggeration or faulty reasoning. The first row has been completed for you as an example.

Ineffective Use of Evidence	Effective Use of Evidence
But for one out of every five children in the world, life is different. This means that billions of children have lived differently since the dawn of time.	But for one out of every five children in the world, life is different. Access to quality education is an issue whose impact should not be ignored.
For instance, over two-thirds of the nearly 800 million illiterate people in the world are women. Therefore, nearly all people in the world who are illiterate are women.	
When gender stereotypes are enforced or allowed in education, they limit girls' access to potentially "lucrative and influential" fields of employment. Women who are subjected to strict gender stereotypes are extremely poor, and all wish they could have careers in STEM fields.	

Please note that excerpts and passages in the StudySync® library and this workbook are intended as touchstones to generate interest in an author's work. The excerpts and passages do not substitute for the reading of entire texts, and StudySync® strongly recommends that students seek out and purchase the whole literary or informational work in order to experience it as the author intended. Links to online resellers are available in our digital library. In addition, complete works may be ordered through an authorized reseller by filling out and returning to StudySync® the order form enclosed in this workbook.

Reading & Writing Companion   137

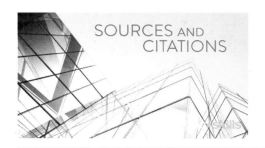

Skill:
Sources and Citations

••• CHECKLIST FOR SOURCES AND CITATIONS

In your oral presentation, provide citations for any information that you obtained from an outside source. This includes the following:

- direct quotations
- paraphrased information
- tables and data
- images
- videos
- audio files

The citations in your presentation should be as brief and unobtrusive as possible. Follow these general guidelines:

- The citation should indicate the author's last name and the page number(s) on which the information appears (if the source has numbered pages), enclosed in parentheses.
- If the author is not known, the citation should list the title of the work and, if helpful, the publisher.

At the end of your presentation, include your works cited list. These are the elements and the order in which they should be listed in works cited entries, according to the MLA style:

- author
- title of source
- container, or the title of the larger work in which the source is located
- other contributors
- version
- number
- publisher
- publication date
- location
- URL, without the "http://"

Not all of these elements will apply to each citation. Include only the elements that are relevant for the source.

To check that you have gathered and cited sources correctly, consider the following questions:

- Did I cite the information I found using a standard format to avoid plagiarism?
- Did I include all my sources in my works cited list?

Please note that excerpts and passages in the StudySync® library and this workbook are intended as touchstones to generate interest in an author's work. The excerpts and passages do not substitute for the reading of entire texts, and StudySync® strongly recommends that students seek out and purchase the whole literary or informational work in order to experience it as the author intended. Links to online resellers are available in our digital library. In addition, complete works may be ordered through an authorized reseller by filling out and returning to StudySync® the order form enclosed in this workbook.

Reading & Writing Companion

139

YOUR TURN

Read the elements and examples below. Then, complete the chart by placing them in the correct order, according to the MLA style for a works cited list. Write the corresponding letter for each element and example in the appropriate column.

	Elements and Examples
A	publisher
B	"Child marriage and education: impacts, costs, and benefits"
C	URL
D	29 June 2017
E	author
F	publication date
G	www.globalpartnership.org/blog/child-marriage-and-education-impacts-costs-and-benefits
H	Global Partnership for Education
I	Wodon, Quentin
J	title of source

Elements	Examples

WRITE

Use the information in the checklist to create or revise your citations and works cited list. Make sure that each slide with researched information briefly identifies the source of the information. This will let your audience know that the information you are presenting is trustworthy. When you have completed your citations, compile a list of all your sources and write out your works cited list. Refer to the *MLA Handbook* as needed.

Skill:
Communicating Ideas

••• CHECKLIST FOR COMMUNICATING IDEAS

Follow these steps as you rehearse your presentation:

- **Eye Contact:** Practice looking up and making eye contact while you speak. Rehearse your presentation in front of a mirror, making eye contact with yourself. Consider choosing a few audience members to look at during your presentation, but scan the audience from time to time so it doesn't seem as if you're speaking directly to only two or three people.

- **Speaking Rate:** Record yourself so you can judge your speaking rate. If you find yourself speaking too fast, time your presentation and work on slowing down your speech. In addition, you might want to plan pauses in your presentation to achieve a specific effect.

- **Volume:** Be aware of your volume. Make sure that you are speaking at a volume that will be loud enough for everyone to hear you, but not so loud that it will be uncomfortable for your audience.

- **Enunciation:** Decide which words you want to emphasize, and then enunciate them with particular clarity. Emphasizing certain words or terms can help you communicate more effectively and drive home your message.

- **Purposeful Gestures:** Rehearse your presentation with your arms relaxed at your sides. If you want to include a specific gesture, decide where in your presentation it will be most effective, and practice making that gesture until it feels natural.

- **Conventions of Language:** Make sure that you are using appropriate conventions of language for your audience and purpose.

⟳ YOUR TURN

Read the examples of students who are communicating their ideas below. Then, complete the chart by first identifying the appropriate category for each example and then deciding whether the example illustrates effective or ineffective communication. Write the corresponding letter for each example in the appropriate place in the chart.

	Examples
A	A student ends his formal presentation by saying, "And that's all I've got for you today, folks!"
B	A student projects his or her voice, but does not shout. He or she pronounces words carefully and speaks at a slightly slower rate than used in normal conversation.
C	A student speaks very softly and rushes through the presentation, using a monotone voice.
D	A student makes eye contact with various members of the audience as well as his or her co-presenters.
E	A student does not look up from his or her notecards.
F	A student uses his or her hands to emphasize a particularly important idea and point to visual aids.
G	A student allows his or her arms to hang limply and does not move at all.
H	A student stands up straight in clear view of his or her audience.
I	A student ends his formal presentation by saying, "Thank you for listening."
J	A student faces a board or screen and stands with his or her arms crossed.

Category	Example of Effective Communication	Example of Ineffective Communication
Posture		
Eye Contact		
Rate/Volume/Enunciation		
Gestures		
Conventions of Language		

✏ WRITE

Take turns delivering your oral presentation in front of a partner.

As you present, do the following:

- Employ steady eye contact with your partner.
- Use an appropriate speaking rate and volume, pauses, and enunciation to clearly communicate with your partner.
- Use natural gestures to add interest and meaning as you speak.
- Maintain a comfortable, confident posture to engage your audience.
- Use language conventions appropriate for a formal presentation, and avoid slang or inappropriate speech.

As you watch your partner's presentation, use the checklist to evaluate his or her communication of ideas.

When you finish giving your presentation, write a brief but honest reflection about your experience of communicating your ideas. Did you make eye contact? Did you speak too quickly or too softly? Did you maintain a comfortable, confident posture? Did you use appropriate language? Did you struggle to incorporate gestures that looked and felt natural? How can you better communicate your ideas in the future?

Skill:
Engaging in Discourse

••• CHECKLIST FOR ENGAGING IN DISCOURSE

You and a partner will take turns practicing your oral presentations and giving feedback. The feedback you provide should be meaningful and respectful. That is, you should offer an honest assessment as well as specific tips for improvement, while using kind and considerate language.

In your feedback, make sure to evaluate and critique the speaker using these categories. Remember to always start by telling the speaker what he or she did particularly well.

Positive Points:

- What is most effective about the oral presentation?
- What strong points does the speaker make?
- Which particular phrases are well written and memorable?

Clarity:

- Does the speaker express his or her ideas in a clear, understandable way?
- What changes can the speaker make to improve the clarity of his or her message?

Coherence:

- Does the speaker use transitions and explanations effectively to show the relationship between ideas?
- Where can the speaker add transitions or explanations to improve the coherence of his or her message?

Diction:

- Does the speaker's choice of words have an impact, or a strong effect?
- Where can the speaker improve his or her word choice to create a stronger impact?

Syntax:

- Does the speaker vary sentence length and complexity to create a strong impact?
- Where can the speaker build techniques, such as parallelism or ending a sentence with the most important idea, into his or her syntax to improve the clarity and impact of the presentation?

Persuasive Techniques:

- Does the speaker use language persuasively?
- Where can the speaker employ specific rhetorical strategies, such as appeals to logic, emotion, and ethics, to more effectively persuade his or her audience?

↻ YOUR TURN

Read the examples of feedback below. Then, complete the chart by placing the examples in the appropriate category. Write the corresponding letter for each example of feedback in the appropriate row. Some examples may belong in more than one category.

	Feedback
A	The transition word *likewise* shows a strong connection between your ideas in this paragraph.
B	I think this sentence would be stronger if you moved the most important phrase to the end.
C	I like how you posed a rhetorical question to engage your audience.
D	I like how you inserted an anecdote to make your presentation more personal and relatable.
E	The wording of this sentence is a little vague. You might consider revising passive sentence constructions.
F	I'm not sure what you were referencing when you said, "as previously discussed." Can you please elaborate?

Category	Feedback
Positive Points	
Clarity	
Coherence	
Diction	
Syntax	
Persuasive Techniques	

WRITE

Take turns reading your presentation aloud to a partner. When you finish, write a reflection about your experience of engaging in discourse by giving feedback. How did you ensure that your feedback was both meaningful and respectful? What did you do well? How can you improve in the future?

Please note that excerpts and passages in the StudySync® library and this workbook are intended as touchstones to generate interest in an author's work. The excerpts and passages do not substitute for the reading of entire texts, and StudySync® strongly recommends that students seek out and purchase the whole literary or informational work in order to experience it as the author intended. Links to online resellers are available in our digital library. In addition, complete works may be ordered through an authorized reseller by filling out and returning to StudySync® the order form enclosed in this workbook.

Reading & Writing Companion   **147**

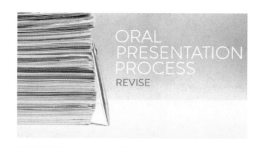

Oral Presentation
Process: Revise

| PLAN | DRAFT | REVISE | EDIT AND PRESENT |

You have written a draft of your argumentative oral presentation. You have also received input from your peers about how to improve it. Now you are going to revise your draft.

◄ REVISION GUIDE

Examine your draft to find areas for revision. Keep in mind your purpose and audience as you revise for clarity, development, organization, and style. Use the guide below to help you review:

Review	Revise	Example
Clarity		
Identify concepts that may need defining or explaining.	Make sure you define or explain key terms that may not be familiar to your audience. Add headings to your presentation slides to clarify your ideas and claims for your audience, and simplify your ideas by turning them into brief bullet points.	The Right to Education Initiative emphasizes the status of education as a "multiplier right," meaning that ensuring a woman's right to education dramatically increases her chances of improving her socioeconomic status by safeguarding "key rights, such as those related to work, property, political participation, access to justice, freedom from violence and health."

Review	Revise	Example
Development		
Identify and annotate places in your presentation where your thesis is not supported by details or evidence.	Make sure you have a strong main idea in each paragraph, and add accurate evidence, examples, well-chosen details, or other supporting information to develop your ideas. Include images, graphs, videos, and other visual elements that support your argument in your presentation.	Many girls are pressured into the labor market at a young age in order to support their families. Instead of getting an education and learning the skills they need for professional employment, ~~Girls~~ girls work in low-skilled jobs for low wages~~.~~, which is detrimental to their health and development. [Project slide with key points listed in bulleted form.]
Organization		
Syntax can help you emphasize ideas. Identify strong words and phrases that show your main ideas.	Revise sentences so that the most important word or phrase comes at the end. Think about places where a visual aid might enhance a section of the presentation.	A lack of education funding in some countries means families are required to pay for any education their child receives. ~~The fees are prohibitive for~~ For many families, especially those living in poor countries~~.~~, the fees are prohibitive.
Style: Word Choice		
Identify key words and phrases that connect ideas across sentences. Annotate places where more precise language would strengthen the connection.	Replace vague or repetitive words and phrases with precise language that emphasizes the connections between your ideas.	The ways in which girls and women worldwide are subjected to discrimination ~~varies widely.~~ cannot be encapsulated by a single narrative. If we are to create justice, we must keep in mind that women all over the world face inequality in different ways.

Review	Revise	Example
Style: Sentence Fluency		
Read your presentation aloud, and listen to the way the text sounds. Does it sound choppy? Or does it flow smoothly with rhythm, movement, and emphasis on important details and events?	Shorten a section of long sentences, or join shorter sentences together using conjunctions or dependent clauses.	This may seem like a tall order. ~~The~~, but the first step is to pay attention to experiences outside of our own. Denying a woman's right to equal education ~~prevents her from living a healthy and fruitful life. Denying a woman's right to equal education~~ is also a denial of her rights to freedom and representation.

✏ WRITE

Another helpful step in the revision process is shortening your draft by trimming and bulleting your draft paragraphs to create more succinct, scannable notes. For example, you might cut information that is overly complex and place it in a list or diagram instead. Make each main idea or point a separate bullet. When delivering your presentation, you can use these notes to remind yourself of the key ideas you want to deliver to your audience.

Use the revision guide and the step described above, as well as your peer reviews, to help you evaluate your oral presentation to determine places that should be revised.

Once you have finished revising your draft, write out your revised oral presentation.

Grammar: Commonly Misspelled Words

By following a few simple steps, you can learn to spell new words—even words that are unfamiliar or difficult. As you write, keep a list of words you have trouble spelling. Refer to online or print resources for pronunciation, Latin or Greek roots, and other information that may help you. Then, use the steps below to learn to spell those words.

Say it. Look at the word again and say it aloud. Say it again, pronouncing each syllable clearly.

See it. Close your eyes. Picture the word. Visualize it letter by letter.

Write it. Look at the word again and write it two or three times. Then, write the word without looking at the printed version.

Check it. Check your spelling. Did you spell it correctly? If not, repeat each step until you can spell it easily.

Here are some words that can sometimes confuse even strong spellers.

Commonly Misspelled Words		
absence	apologetically	answer
accessible	caricature	connoisseur
cruelty	detrimental	devastation
division	exhilaration	exist
exuberant	fascism	fundamentally
genius	humorous	hypocrite
ideally	intellectual	leisurely
malicious	maneuver	negotiable
neighborhood	newsstand	possessed
salable	restaurant	synonymous

Please note that excerpts and passages in the StudySync® library and this workbook are intended as touchstones to generate interest in an author's work. The excerpts and passages do not substitute for the reading of entire texts, and StudySync® strongly recommends that students seek out and purchase the whole literary or informational work in order to experience it as the author intended. Links to online resellers are available in our digital library. In addition, complete works may be ordered through an authorized reseller by filling out and returning to StudySync® the order form enclosed in this workbook.

Reading & Writing Companion

151

↻ YOUR TURN

1. How should this sentence be changed?

   > Each morning Mr. Fritts takes a liesurely walk to his favorite newsstand and buys a paper.

   - ○ A. Change **liesurely** to **leisurly** and newsstand to **newstand.**
   - ○ B. Change **liesurely** to **leisurely.**
   - ○ C. Change **liesurely** to **leisiurely.**
   - ○ D. No change needs to be made to this sentence.

2. How should this sentence be changed?

   > Ideally, the florist for the wedding will be a true conoiseur of color, scent, and space.

   - ○ A. Change **Ideally** to **Idealy.**
   - ○ B. Change **conoiseur** to **connoisure.**
   - ○ C. Change **conoiseur** to **connoisseur.**
   - ○ D. No change needs to be made to this sentence.

3. How should this sentence be changed?

   > Some people think Eddie is malicous, but I know he is just exhuberant.

   - ○ A. Change **malicous** to **malicious** and **exhuberant** to **exuberant.**
   - ○ B. Change **exhuberant** to **exuberent.**
   - ○ C. Change **malicous** to **malischious.**
   - ○ D. No change needs to be made to this sentence.

4. How should this sentence be changed?

   > Ms. Peabody's fourth grade class loves that particular book because it is both humorous and accessible.

   - ○ A. Change **humorous** to **humerous.**
   - ○ B. Change **humorous** to **humorus** and **accessible** to **accesible.**
   - ○ C. Change **accessible** to **acessible.**
   - ○ D. No change needs to be made to this sentence.

Grammar:
Sentence Variety - Openings

Sentence Openers

Sentence openers introduce and connect ideas. Openers can be single words or phrases and can function as different parts of speech that describe or indicate time or place or show similarity, contrast, cause or effect, and other connections with surrounding sentences. Using a variety of sentence openers throughout your writing keeps the reader engaged and helps the flow of ideas from sentence to sentence. Avoid the repetition of syntax and diction as that encourages the repetition of common sentence openers. Combine the use of these additional strategies when beginning sentences:

Strategies	Text
Use a prepositional phrase to begin a sentence.	With blasphemous oaths, he called me a black liar, a runaway from Georgia, and every other profane and vulgar epithet that the most indecent fancy could conceive. 12 Years a Slave
Use an adverb to begin a sentence.	Implicitly, it accepted the position of Northern Ireland within the United Kingdom. A Brief History of Ireland
Use a very short sentence, which can help emphasize an important point or create excitement.	We can do that. A More Perfect Union
Use transitional words (showing cause and effect, similarities or differences, etc.) to begin a sentence.	By the same token, a just law is a code that a majority compels a minority to follow and that it is willing to follow itself. Letter from Birmingham Jail
Use words that indicate time or a sequence of events to begin a sentence.	Soon after nine o'clock of a Saturday morning, kids began spraying out of all the side streets on to Manhattan Avenue, the main thoroughfare. A Tree Grows in Brooklyn

↻ YOUR TURN

1. How should this sentence be changed to use a causal transition as a sentence opener?

> Many people were left without power for 48 hours.

- ○ A. Frighteningly, many people were left without power for 48 hours.
- ○ B. As a result, many people were left without power for 48 hours.
- ○ C. In rural areas, many people were left without power for 48 hours.
- ○ D. No change needs to be made to this sentence.

2. How should this sentence be changed to use an adverb as a sentence opener?

> Thankfully, my hard work paid off.

- ○ A. My hard work paid off, thankfully.
- ○ B. I am thankful that my hard work paid off.
- ○ C. My hard work thankfully paid off.
- ○ D. No change needs to be made to this sentence.

3. How should this sentence be changed to make the sentence opener clearer?

> Bats live in cities.

- ○ A. Cities are places that bats live.
- ○ B. The bats live in cities.
- ○ C. Many bats live in cities.
- ○ D. No change needs to be made to this sentence.

4. How should this sentence be changed to use a time transition as a sentence opener?

> Clemens began using the pen name Mark Twain and started writing for the *Enterprise* in Virginia City.

- ○ A. Mark Twain started writing for the *Enterprise* soon after.
- ○ B. Surprisingly, Samuel Clemens started writing for the *Enterprise* in Virginia City.
- ○ C. Soon Clemens, who had begun using the pen name Mark Twain, was writing for the *Enterprise* in Virginia City.
- ○ D. No change needs to be made to this sentence.

Grammar:
Sentence Variety - Length

Like an interesting conversation, writing should engage the reader. Using varied and rhythmic sentence length and syntax injects more interest into your writing. Varying your syntax and sentence length will help emphasize important pieces of information, enhance descriptions and narratives, and reduce repetition. The strategies in this lesson are useful in any type of writing.

Strategy	Text
Vary the rhythm by alternating short and long sentences.	Anyway, Ashley finishes her story and then goes around the room and asks everyone else why they're supporting the campaign. They all have different stories and reasons. Many bring up a specific issue. And finally they come to this elderly black man who's been sitting there quietly the entire time. And Ashley asks him why he's there. And he does not bring up a specific issue. A More Perfect Union
Use simple, compound, complex, and compound-complex sentences to vary syntax and sentence length.	It was no use trying the lift. Even at the best of times it was seldom working, and at present the electric current was cut off during daylight hours. It was part of the economy drive in preparation for Hate Week. The flat was seven flights up, and Winston, who was thirty-nine and had a varicose ulcer above his right ankle, went slowly, resting several times on the way. 1984
Use different sentence openers to encourage sentence variety.	And I love Havana, its noise and decay and painted ladyness. I could happily sit on one of those wrought-iron balconies for days, or keep my grandmother company on her porch, with its ringside view of the sea. I'm afraid to lose all this. To lose Abuela Celia again. But I know that sooner or later I'd have to return to New York. Dreaming in Cuban
Use different sentence types, including imperative, interrogative, and exclamatory sentences, to help vary length.	And today, I want just to take a moment once again to look around this beautiful auditorium at the people who helped you on your journey—your families and friends, everyone in your school and your communities—all the people who pushed you and poured their love into you and believed in you even when you didn't believe in yourselves sometimes. Today is their day, too, right? So let's, graduates, give them a big, old, loud shout-out and love to our families. Thank you all. Yes! Commencement Address to the Santa Fe Indian School

↻ YOUR TURN

1. How was the sample sentence edited to become longer?

> Sample Sentence: The kitten caught the butterfly.
>
> Edited Sentence: Leaping into the air, the kitten caught the butterfly.

- ○ A. The sample sentence was changed to a compound sentence.
- ○ B. The sample sentence was changed to a compound-complex sentence.
- ○ C. The sample sentence was changed to use a participial phrase as a sentence opener.
- ○ D. The sample sentence was changed to use an adverb as a sentence opener.

2. How was the sample sentence edited to become longer?

> Sample Sentence: Jason stared at his feet.
>
> Edited Sentence: While thinking of an answer, Jason stared at his feet.

- ○ A. The sample sentence was changed to add a phrase as a sentence opener.
- ○ B. The sample sentence was changed to an imperative sentence.
- ○ C. The sample sentence was changed to a compound-complex sentence.
- ○ D. The sample sentence was changed to include a verb as a sentence opener.

3. How can this sentence be shortened and correctly edited to create a complex sentence?

> If this snow continues, school will be canceled, and we'll have to stay home.

- ○ A. Remove **If this snow continues,** and capitalize **school.**
- ○ B. Replace the second comma with a period and remove **and we'll have to stay home.**
- ○ C. Replace the second comma and the conjunction **and** with a semicolon.
- ○ D. Replace the first comma with a semicolon and remove **school will be canceled, and.**

4. How can this sentence be changed into a compound-complex sentence, effectively making it longer?

> When small children are really tired, they are short-tempered.

- ○ A. Remove the period and add *until they fall asleep.* after **short-tempered.**
- ○ B. Replace the comma with a semicolon.
- ○ C. Change the period after **short-tempered** to a semicolon and add *some will cry and fuss.*
- ○ D. Remove the comma.

Oral Presentation Process:
Edit and Present

PLAN	DRAFT	REVISE	EDIT AND PRESENT

You have revised your oral presentation based on your peer feedback and your own examination.

Now, it is time to edit your argumentative oral presentation. When you revised, you focused on the content of your oral presentation. You practiced strategies for communicating your ideas and engaging in discourse. When you edit, you focus on the mechanics of your oral presentation, paying close attention to standard English conventions that can be heard by your audience while you are talking.

Use the checklist below to guide you as you edit:

☐ Are there sentences that are too long and hard to follow? Can I use different sentence types to vary the length of sentences?

☐ Have I used punctuation such as periods, commas, colons, and semicolons correctly to indicate pauses for effect?

☐ Have I included a variety of sentence openers in my presentation?

☐ Have I correctly spelled all words?

☐ Have I used any language that is too informal for my presentation?

☐ Have I added visual aids and digital media strategically to enhance my presentation?

Notice some edits Susie has made:

- Changed a sentence opener to better engage her audience

- Replaced slang or informal language with formal language

- Corrected a commonly misspelled word

- Added rhetorical questions to vary sentence types

Please note that excerpts and passages in the StudySync® library and this workbook are intended as touchstones to generate interest in an author's work. The excerpts and passages do not substitute for the reading of entire texts, and StudySync® strongly recommends that students seek out and purchase the whole literary or informational work in order to experience it as the author intended. Links to online resellers are available in our digital library. In addition, complete works may be ordered through an authorized reseller by filling out and returning to StudySync® the order form enclosed in this workbook.

Reading & Writing Companion   **157**

[Title slide.] On mornings when frost covers our windows, the hot sun begs us outside, or we're exhausted from a restless night, ~~Sometimes~~ going to school is ~~a bummer~~ the last thing we want to do. It's easy to take school for granted when its doors are wide open to us. But for one out of every five children ~~globaly~~ globally, life is different. One-hundred thirty million girls worldwide are not in school ("Girls' education"). Imagine if you never had the choice to step foot into a classroom. Where would you be today? What kind of opportunities and future could you look forward to?

✏ WRITE

After Susie rehearses her presentation, she decides to edit her introduction further by dividing up her points. In addition, she decides to help her audience visualize some of the information in her introduction by including a slide with a graphic.

Use the checklist, as well as your peer reviews, to help you evaluate your oral presentation to determine places that need editing. Then, edit your presentation to correct those errors. Finally, rehearse your presentation, including both the delivery of your written work and the strategic use of the visual aids and digital media you plan to incorporate.

Once you have made all your corrections and rehearsed with your digital media selections, you are ready to present your work. You may present to your class or to a group of your peers. You can record your presentation to share with family and friends or post it on your blog. If you publish online, share the link with your family, friends, and classmates.

The Landscape of Being Here for You

DRAMA

Introduction

In this short play, a young man finds himself alone and struggling to care for his dying father. The young man feels like everyone has abandoned him and his father. Now overwhelmed from stress, exhaustion, and isolation, will the young man choose to abandon his father, too?

VOCABULARY

sound

to communicate a specific impression, particularly when heard

obvious

easy to notice or understand

professional

acting in a way that is appropriate for a job

vision

seeing

bond

a feeling that keeps people together

NOTES

≡ READ

1 [SCENE: The stage is divided into three small sets. The first set is stage left and has a mirror suspended over a sink with a small shelf beside it. The second set is center stage and has a sofa facing a recliner with a small chair between them. The third set is stage right and has a water cooler with three foldable chairs near it. LUCAS stands at the front edge of the stage, watching DAD sleep in the recliner.]

2 LUCAS: (turning to face the audience) That's my father. He's in the living room of his house. He's asleep right now—a rare moment of peace. You'd think I would be able to enjoy the quiet, but my thoughts are too rowdy. You know how thoughts can be.

3 (speeding up his speech to imitate how his thoughts **sound** in his head)

4 People are talking about you, gossiping about you, talking about you, gossiping about you. Talking about you, gossiping about you.

5   (*in normal speech again*)

6   That's how it sounds in my head. (*pause*) People do talk about me. They talk about how I'm never at work anymore, and when I do show up, how I'm always late. They think it's because I drink.too much at night.

7   (*KAYLA, DANA, and RON walk onto the set with the water cooler. They sit.*)

8   KAYLA: You know he drinks way too much.

9   RON: How do you know that?

10   DANA: Come on, Ron. It's obvious. He's hardly ever at work. He's always late.

11   KAYLA: Right. And he never looks **professional** like us. He always has messy hair, wrinkled clothes. Sometimes I don't think he even knows what a razor is.

12   DANA: He used to be so clean cut. A real handsome guy.

13   RON: I guess you're right. That's what happens when you drink too much.

14   LUCAS: (*to the audience*) Of course, it's not true. But it gives them something to focus on; it gives them something in common. It serves as an unseemly **bond** for their friendship. I don't have time for it, but it still bothers me. So in my head, my thoughts try to keep me calm.

15   (*speeding up his speech to imitate his thoughts*)
16   Don't stress out. Don't stress out. Don't stress out. Don't stress out.

17   (*in a normal speech again*)
18   Last week, they found out the truth. Did it stop them? No. They still gossip. I think that gossiping about me comforts them. It has become too much of a ritual for them, and the truth only serves as something to twist.

19   (*KAYLA, DANA, and RON talk in low voices and pause at times to look disapprovingly at Lucas. The audience can't hear what they are saying. But it is* **obvious** *by their looks that they are gossiping about Lucas.*)

20   LUCAS: In my head I hear my thoughts.

21   (*speeding up his speech to imitate his thoughts*)
22   Don't worry about them. Don't worry about them. Don't worry about them. Don't worry. Don't worry. Don't worry.

23   (*in a normal speech again*)

Please note that excerpts and passages in the StudySync® library and this workbook are intended as touchstones to generate interest in an author's work. The excerpts and passages do not substitute for the reading of entire texts, and StudySync® strongly recommends that students seek out and purchase the whole literary or informational work in order to experience it as the author intended. Links to online resellers are available in our digital library. In addition, complete works may be ordered through an authorized reseller by filling out and returning to StudySync® the order form enclosed in this workbook.

Reading & Writing Companion   **161**

NOTES

24 But who wouldn't worry? They complicate my life. One day they got too worked up over my situation, and they made a call.

25 KAYLA (*on a smartphone in the office set*) Social Services? You better get over to that house now.

26 (*There's a LOUD KNOCK at the door. DAD wakes up. LUCAS walks to the back of the living room, and a SOCIAL WORKER nearly runs over him as she enters. She sits in the chair. LUCAS remains standing.*)

27 SOCIAL WORKER: (*cold and clinical*) I'm checking in to make sure everything is fine. Would you please sit down?

28 LUCAS: (*to the audience*) Give me a break! That's what I want to shout at her. How could everything be fine?

29 SOCIAL WORKER: Are you taking care of your father? Are you feeding him? Someone has filed a report.

30 (*LUCAS slowly walks to the edge of the stage as the SOCIAL WORKER continues talking.*)

31 SOCIAL WORKER: Are you taking your father to see the doctors? Do you leave him alone? Do you drink?

32 LUCAS: (*to the audience*) If she would only take a moment to look around her, she would never ask those hurtful questions. She doesn't have time to truly be here though; no one has time.

33 (*The living room set goes dim as the SOCIAL WORKER leaves.*)

34 LUCAS: (*to the audience*) If people want to know the truth, they can ask, up front and direct. Here's the truth—my father is dying. I'm exhausted. My body and my heart hurt. Friends have stopped calling. The doctors have given up. I'm the only one left for my father.

35 (*LUCAS pauses to watch his father sleeping in his recliner.*)

36 LUCAS: (*to the audience*) No one knows how real family works. They don't know what it is like to be there for him when everyone else has turned away. They don't get how it rips out your heart, how it makes you crazy for someone to talk to, for someone to listen, for someone simply to be with you because you're scared.

37   KAYLA: (*from the office set*) That Lucas needs to grow up!

38   (*LUCAS goes to DAD and helps him stand up, steadying him as they start to walk to the sink.*)

39   LUCAS: (*to the audience while he's walking with DAD*) My father is six feet two inches tall; however, he only weighs 140 pounds. He was a Marine. He used to be strong and proud. Now he's frail and unable to walk without help.

40   (*LUCAS and DAD arrive at the sink.*)

41   DAD: (*looking in the mirror*) Hand me my brush.

42   (*LUCAS hands DAD the brush from the shelf. DAD takes the brush and makes faces in the mirror to try to focus his **vision**. Then DAD carefully parts his hair to the right. As he finishes, DAD hands the brush to LUCAS, who returns it to the shelf. DAD studies himself in the mirror.*)

43   LUCAS: (*to the audience*) Can you see him? He's still looking at himself in the mirror—studying his face, his chest, his arms. (*watching DAD*) Can you see the face that he makes in the mirror? It's a mix of disgust and surprise and sadness.

44   DAD: Look at me. I'm so skinny.

45   (*LUCAS walks to the edge of the stage.*)

46   LUCAS: (*to the audience*) I can feel it all. The skinny, bony body of my father, the Marine, and the look he gives himself. I feel it in my heart, and my heart breaks. (*pause*) It's a new world now—a different landscape under our feet.

47   (*LUCAS starts to walk back to DAD. After a few steps, LUCAS pauses and turns again to the audience.*)

48   LUCAS: (*to the audience*) I say nothing to my father when he notices how skinny he is. Saying anything at all would be saying something for me, something to try to soothe my hurt. It would steal the moment from him. Instead, I stay with him—silent—so he can stay with himself in his disgust, in his surprise, and in his sadness.

49   (*LUCAS walks to DAD.*)

50   I place my hands on his shoulders. And without a single word, he knows that I am here for him.

51   (*The stage goes dark.*)

First Read

Read "The Landscape of Being Here for You." After you read, complete the Think Questions below.

☁ THINK QUESTIONS

1. According to Lucas's coworkers, why does he miss so much time from work?

   _____

   _____

2. What is the real reason Lucas misses so much time from work?

   _____

   _____

3. According to Lucas, what do people not understand about his situation? Include evidence from the text to support your response.

   _____

   _____

4. Use context to confirm the meaning of the word *bond* as it is used in "The Landscape of Being Here for You." Write your definition of *bond* here.

   Bond means _____

   A context clue is _____

5. What is another way to say that it is obvious that the coworkers are *gossiping* about Lucas?

   Coworkers are _____

   _____

Skill:
Analyzing Expressions

★ DEFINE

When you read, you may find English expressions that you do not know. An **expression** is a group of words that communicates an idea. Three types of expressions are idioms, sayings, and figurative language. They can be difficult to understand because the meanings of the words are different from their **literal,** or usual, meanings.

An **idiom** is an expression that is commonly known among a group of people. For example, "It's raining cats and dogs" means it is raining heavily. **Sayings** are short expressions that contain advice or wisdom. For instance, "Don't count your chickens before they hatch" means do not plan on something good happening before it happens. **Figurative** language is when you describe something by comparing it with something else, either directly (using the words *like* or *as*) or indirectly. For example, "I'm as hungry as a horse" means I'm very hungry. None of the expressions are about actual animals.

••• CHECKLIST FOR ANALYZING EXPRESSIONS

To determine the meaning of an expression, remember the following:

✓ If you find a confusing group of words, it may be an expression. The meaning of words in expressions may not be their literal meaning.

- Ask yourself: Is this confusing because the words are new? Or because the words do not make sense together?

✓ Determining the overall meaning may require that you use one or more of the following:

- context clues

- a dictionary or other resource

- teacher or peer support

✓ Highlight important information before and after the expression to look for clues.

⟳ YOUR TURN

Read the excerpts and the literal meaning of each boldface expression below. Then, complete the chart by identifying the meaning of each expression as it is used in the text

Meaning in the Text Options	
A	to hurt someone emotionally
B	to act responsibly like an adult
C	to disbelieve what someone says

Excerpt	Literal Meaning	Meaning in the Text
LUCAS: (*to the audience*) **Give me a break**! That's what I want to shout at her. How could everything be fine?	to give someone time to rest from work	
LUCAS: (*to the audience*) No one knows how real family works. They don't know what it is like to be there for him when everyone else has turned away. They don't get how it **rips out your heart**, how it makes you crazy for someone to talk to, for someone to listen, for someone simply to be with you because you're scared.	to pull the heart out of the body	
KAYLA: (*from the office set*) That Lucas needs to **grow up**!	to age from a child to an adult	

Skill: Analyzing and Evaluating Text

★ DEFINE

Analyzing and **evaluating** a text means reading carefully to understand the author's **purpose** and **message**. In informational texts, authors may provide information or opinions on a topic. They may be writing to inform or persuade a reader. In fictional texts, the author may be **communicating** a message or lesson through their story. They may write to entertain, or to teach the reader something about life.

Sometimes authors are clear about their message and purpose. When the message or purpose is not stated directly, readers will need to look closer at the text. Readers can use textual evidence to make inferences about what the author is trying to communicate. By analyzing and evaluating the text, you can form your own thoughts and opinions about what you read.

••• CHECKLIST FOR ANALYZING AND EVALUATING TEXT

In order to analyze and evaluate a text, do the following:

✓ Look for details that show why the author is writing.

- Ask yourself: Is the author trying to inform, persuade, or entertain? What are the main ideas of this text?

✓ Look for details that show what the author is trying to say.

- Ask yourself: What is the author's opinion about this topic? Is there a lesson I can learn from this story?

✓ Form your own thoughts and opinions about the text.

- Ask yourself: Do I agree with the author? Does this message apply to my life?

Please note that excerpts and passages in the StudySync® library and this workbook are intended as touchstones to generate interest in an author's work. The excerpts and passages do not substitute for the reading of entire texts, and StudySync® strongly recommends that students seek out and purchase the whole literary or informational work in order to experience it as the author intended. Links to online resellers are available in our digital library. In addition, complete works may be ordered through an authorized reseller by filling out and returning to StudySync® the order form enclosed in this workbook.

Reading & Writing Companion   **167**

♻ YOUR TURN

Read lines 31–34 from "The Landscape of Being Here for You." Then, using the Checklist on the previous page, answer the multiple-choice questions below.

---

from "The Landscape of Being Here for You"

SOCIAL WORKER: Are you taking your father to see the doctors? Do you leave him alone? Do you drink?

LUCAS: (*to the audience*) If she would only take a moment to look around her, she would never ask those hurtful questions. She doesn't have time to truly be here though; no one has time.

(*The living room set goes dim as the SOCIAL WORKER leaves.*)

LUCAS: (*to the audience*) If people want to know the truth, they can ask, up front and direct. Here's the truth—my father is dying. I'm exhausted. My body and my heart hurt. Friends have stopped calling. The doctors have given up. I'm the only one left for my father.

---

1. What message is the author trying to show in the excerpt?

   ○ A. Social workers are mean people.
   ○ B. People often forget or stop caring about caregivers and those they care for.
   ○ C. Parents don't have time for their children.
   ○ D. Lucas's father is dying.

2. What textual evidence helped you infer this?

   ○ A. "If she would only take a moment to look around her, she would never ask those hurtful questions."
   ○ B. "(*The living room set goes dim as the SOCIAL WORKER leaves.*)"
   ○ C. "I'm exhausted. My body and my heart hurt."
   ○ D. "I'm the only one left for my father."

THE LANDSCAPE OF BEING HERE FOR YOU

Close Read

✏ WRITE

NARRATIVE: In this play, the experience of caring for a dying father is a source of conflict and an opportunity for new understanding. Select a character, and describe an event in the play from his or her point of view using details from the text. How does your character feel? What does he or she think? What new understanding or lesson might he or she learn? Pay attention to homophones as you write.

Use the checklist below to guide you as you write.

☐ What does your character do during the scene?

☐ What emotions does your character experience during the scene?

☐ What does your character think about the situation?

☐ What lesson might your character learn?

Use the sentence frames to organize and write your narrative.

In the play, I am _____.

When I _____, I _____.

I feel _____.

But I know that I have to _____.

If I try (to / too / two) _____ understand what is really happening, I can learn a lesson.

The lesson I can learn is _____

_____.

Please note that excerpts and passages in the StudySync® library and this workbook are intended as touchstones to generate interest in an author's work. The excerpts and passages do not substitute for the reading of entire texts, and StudySync® strongly recommends that students seek out and purchase the whole literary or informational work in order to experience it as the author intended. Links to online resellers are available in our digital library. In addition, complete works may be ordered through an authorized reseller by filling out and returning to StudySync® the order form enclosed in this workbook.

Reading & Writing Companion   **169**

The Quest for Woman Suffrage

INFORMATIONAL TEXT

Introduction

American women in the 19th century were denied many rights, including suffrage, or the right to vote in political elections. This nonfiction article focuses on two Americans who played a significant role in the quest for woman suffrage: Elizabeth Cady Stanton and Susan B. Anthony. The article describes Stanton and Anthony's efforts to help American women achieve suffrage and the organization that they created for this purpose.

ⓥ VOCABULARY

advocate
show support for an idea or a person

uncompromising
not wanting to change an idea, a belief, or an opinion

disfranchised
kept from having certain rights, particularly the right to vote

ratify
to officially or legally approve

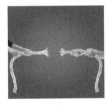

schism
a separation between members of a group caused by a disagreement

suffragist
a person who works to give voting rights to a group that lacks them

☰ READ

NOTES

1 In the 19th century, women in the United States lacked many rights. Married women could not own property or keep the money they earned. Women could not practice law or medicine. Women also did not have the right to vote—a right called woman suffrage. Many thought that women were too fragile to participate in politics. U.S. politician Daniel Webster said, "The rough contests of the political world are not suited to the dignity and delicacy" of women.

2 Elizabeth Cady Stanton and Susan B. Anthony began to **advocate** for women's rights. They worked tirelessly to help women gain the right to vote. In 1866, Stanton and Anthony helped form the American Equal Rights Association (AERA). The AERA aimed to secure voting rights for both women and African American men. AERA members could not decide whether to support the proposed 15th Amendment to the U.S. Constitution. This amendment would give African American men, but not women of any race, the right to vote. It read, "The right of citizens of the United States to vote shall not be denied or abridged by the United States or by any State on account of race, color, or previous condition of servitude." Nowhere did it mention women.

NOTES

3   The exclusion of women from the 15th Amendment angered Stanton and Anthony. Stanton noted, "So long as there is a **disfranchised** class in this country, and that class is women, a man's government is worse than a white man's government. . . ." In other words, women would suffer even more if all men could vote but women could not. Anthony stated, "I would sooner cut off my right hand than ask the ballot for the black man and not for woman."

4   This **schism** in the AERA led Stanton and Anthony to form the National Woman Suffrage Association (NWSA) in May 1869. The NWSA opposed the 15th Amendment because it excluded women. The group's bold motto was "Men, their rights and nothing more; Women, their rights and nothing less." The organization's ambitious goals were to achieve suffrage through a new amendment to the U.S. Constitution that included women, and to expand women's economic and social rights.

5   In November 1869, Lucy Stone and other former AERA members created the American Woman Suffrage Association (AWSA). Stone said that the AWSA was created "to unite those who cannot use the methods which Mrs. Stanton and Susan use." This statement revealed her distaste for her rivals' **uncompromising** approach to suffrage. Like the NWSA, the AWSA aimed to secure voting rights for American women. Unlike the NWSA, the AWSA supported the 15th Amendment, focused only on suffrage, and worked to achieve suffrage through changes to state laws, not the U.S. Constitution.

6   Women were never added to the 15th Amendment, which was **ratified** in 1870. However, the NWSA continued its quest for suffrage. Anthony traveled widely, giving impressive speeches and advising other **suffragists**. She was arrested for voting illegally in the 1872 presidential election. At her trial, Anthony said, "The only chance women have for justice in this country is to violate the law, as I have done, and as I shall continue to do." She was convicted and ordered to pay a fine. She refused to do so.

7   Anthony wisely realized that suffrage would not happen as long as the movement was divided. Thus, the NWSA joined with the AWSA in 1890 to become the National American Woman Suffrage Association (NAWSA). NAWSA worked to achieve suffrage by getting enough state amendments ratified to make Congress approve a new amendment to the U.S. Constitution.

8   Neither Stanton nor Anthony would live to see women get the right to vote. However, the goal of suffrage was achieved in 1920, when the 19th Amendment to the U.S. Constitution was ratified: "The right of citizens of the United States to vote shall not be denied or abridged by the United States or by any State on account of sex."

First Read

Read "The Quest for Woman Suffrage." After you read, complete the Think Questions below.

1. What is woman suffrage?

    Woman suffrage is _____ .

2. Why did Elizabeth Cady Stanton and Susan B. Anthony not support the proposed 15th Amendment to the U.S. Constitution?

    Elizabeth Cady Stanton and Susan B. Anthony did not support the 15th Amendment because _____

    _____ .

3. Why did Susan B. Anthony and her organization NWSA decide to work with Lucy Stone's organization AWSA?

    Susan B. Anthony and NWSA decided to work with Lucy Stone and AWSA because _____

    _____ .

4. Use context to determine the meaning of the word *disfranchised* as it is used in "The Quest for Woman Suffrage." Write your definition of *disfranchised* here.

    Disfranchised means _____ .

    A context clue is _____ .

5. What is another way of saying the states *ratified* the new amendment?

    The states _____

    _____ .

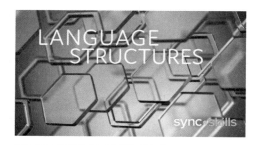

Skill:
Language Structures

★ DEFINE

In every language, there are rules that tell how to **structure** sentences. These rules define the correct order of words. In the English language, for example, a **basic** structure for sentences is subject, verb, and object. Some sentences have more **complicated** structures.

You will encounter both basic and complicated **language structures** in the classroom materials you read. Being familiar with language structures will help you better understand the text.

••• CHECKLIST FOR LANGUAGE STRUCTURES

To improve your comprehension of language structures, do the following:

✓ Monitor your understanding.

- Ask yourself: Why do I not understand this sentence? Is it because the sentence is long? Or is it because I do not understand the logical relationship between ideas in this sentence?

✓ Pay attention to coordinating conjunctions.

- **Coordinating conjunctions** show an equal emphasis on the ideas in a sentence.
- Some examples of coordinating conjunctions are *and*, *but*, and *or*.

✓ Pay attention to subordinating conjunctions.

- **Subordinating conjunctions** show that one idea is more important and the other idea is less important, or subordinate.
- Some examples of subordinating conjunctions are *after*, *instead*, and *once*.

✓ Break down the sentence into its parts.

- Ask yourself: How does the writer use conjunctions to combine sentences? Can I break the sentence vdown into two shorter sentences?

✓ Confirm your understanding with a peer or teacher.

⟳ YOUR TURN

Read paragraph 6 from "The Quest for Woman Suffrage." Then, using the Checklist on the previous page, answer the multiple-choice questions below.

---

from "The Quest for Woman Suffrage"

(1) Women were never added to the 15th Amendment, which was ratified in 1870. (2) However, the NWSA continued its quest for suffrage. (3) Anthony traveled widely, giving impressive speeches and advising other suffragists. (4) She was arrested for voting illegally in the 1872 presidential election. (5) At her trial, Anthony said, "The only chance women have for justice in this country is to violate the law, as I have done, and as I shall continue to do." (6) She was convicted and ordered to pay a fine. (7) She refused to do so.

---

1. Which sentences use coordinating conjunctions?

   ○ A. sentences 1 and 2
   ○ B. sentences 2 and 4
   ○ C. sentences 3 and 6
   ○ D. sentences 4 and 5

2. What is the subordinating conjunction in sentence 1?

   ○ A. Women
   ○ B. never
   ○ C. to
   ○ D. which

3. Which of the following sentences uses a conjunction to connect equally important ideas?

   ○ A. She was convicted and ordered to pay a fine because she refused to do so.
   ○ B. Although she was convicted and ordered to pay a fine, she refused to do so.
   ○ C. She was convicted and ordered to pay a fine, but she refused to do so.
   ○ D. After she was convicted and ordered to pay a fine, she refused to do so.

Skill:
Comparing and Contrasting

Copyright © BookheadEd Learning, LLC

★ DEFINE

To **compare** is to show how two or more pieces of information or literary elements in a text are similar. To **contrast** is to show how two or more pieces of information or literary elements in a text are different. By comparing and contrasting, you can better understand the **meaning** and the **purpose** of the text you are reading.

••• CHECKLIST FOR COMPARING AND CONTRASTING

In order to compare and contrast, do the following:

✓ Look for information or elements that you can compare and contrast.

- Ask yourself: How are these two things similar? How are they different?

✓ Look for signal words that indicate a compare-and-contrast relationship.

- Ask yourself: Are there any words that indicate the writer is trying to compare and contrast two or more things?

✓ Use a graphic organizer, such as a Venn diagram or chart, to compare and contrast information.

YOUR TURN

Read paragraphs 4 and 5 from "The Quest for Woman Suffrage." Then, using the Checklist on the previous page, complete the chart below to compare and contrast the passages.

---

from "The Quest for Woman Suffrage"

This schism in the AERA led Stanton and Anthony to form the National Woman Suffrage Association (NWSA) in May 1869. The NWSA opposed the 15th Amendment because it excluded women. The group's bold motto was "Men, their rights and nothing more; Women, their rights and nothing less." The organization's ambitious goals were to achieve suffrage through a new amendment to the U.S. Constitution that included women, and to expand women's economic and social rights.

In November 1869, Lucy Stone and other former AERA members created the American Woman Suffrage Association (AWSA). Stone said that the AWSA was created "to unite those who cannot use the methods which Mrs. Stanton and Susan use." This statement revealed her distaste for her rivals' uncompromising approach to suffrage. Like the NWSA, the AWSA aimed to secure voting rights for American women. Unlike the NWSA, the AWSA supported the 15th Amendment, focused only on suffrage, and worked to achieve suffrage through changes to state laws, not the U.S. Constitution.

	Observations and Details
A	formed by former AERA members
B	worked toward gaining voting rights for women through state laws
C	opposed the 15th Amendment
D	supported the 15th Amendment
E	fought for a new amendment to the U.S. Constitution that included all men and women
F	fought to gain voting rights for women

Please note that excerpts and passages in the StudySync® library and this workbook are intended as touchstones to generate interest in an author's work. The excerpts and passages do not substitute for the reading of entire texts, and StudySync® strongly recommends that students seek out and purchase the whole literary or informational work in order to experience it as the author intended. Links to online resellers are available in our digital library. In addition, complete works may be ordered through an authorized reseller by filling out and returning to StudySync® the order form enclosed in this workbook.

Reading & Writing Companion 177

NWSA	Both	AWSA

Close Read

✏️ **WRITE**

INFORMATIVE: How did Susan B. Anthony both divide and unite women in the fight for the right to vote? Write a short paragraph in which you explain her unique role in the quest for woman suffrage. Use details from the text to support your explanation. Pay attention to and edit for the possessive case.

Use the checklist below to guide you as you write.

☐ What did Susan B. Anthony do that united women?

☐ What did Susan B. Anthony do that divided women?

☐ What did Susan B. Anthony do to continue her fight for woman suffrage?

Use the sentence frames to organize and write your narrative.

Susan B. Anthony believed that women should have the right to vote. She _____

women by helping to create the _____

and fighting for _____ right to vote. She _____ women

when she _____ the 15th Amendment.

This caused some women to leave the AERA. Susan B. Anthony formed the _____

to continue fighting for woman suffrage.

PHOTO/IMAGE CREDITS:

cover - ©iStock.com/serts
cover - ©iStock.com/eyewave, iStock.com/subjug, ©iStock.com/Ivantsov, iStock.com/borchee, ©iStock.com/seb_ra
p. iii, iStock.com/DNY59
p. iv, ©iStock.com/Blackbeck
p. iv, Kate Chopin - Public Domain
p. v, ©iStock.com/Blackbeck
p. v, iStock.com/LdF
p. vi, ©iStock.com/Blackbeck
p. vi, istock.com/fcafotodigital
p. vi, Stock.com/stanley45/
p. vi, iStock.com/Dean Mitchell
p. vi, iStock.com/Wavebreakmedia
p. vi, iStock.com/Rich Legg
p. vii, iStock.com/hanibaram, iStock.com/seb_ra, iStock.com/Martin Barraud
p. vii, iStock.com/oonal
p. ix, ©iStock.com/serts
p. x, Chimamanda Ngozi Adichie - Taylor Hill/Contributor/FilmMagic/Getty Images
p. x, Rita Dove - Getty Images Europe: Barbara Zanon/Contributor
p. x, Ralph Waldo Ellison - Everett Collection Historical/Alamy Stock Photo
p. x, Louise Erdrich - Ulf Andersen/Contributor/Getty Images Entertainment
p. x, Skip Hollandsworth - Michael Buckner/Staff/Getty Images Entertainment
p. xi, Martin Luther King Jr. - Bettmann/Contributor/Bettmann/Getty Images
p. xi, Abraham Lincoln - Bettmann/Contributor/Bettmann/Getty Images
p. xi, Aimee Nezhukumatahil - Used by permission of Aimee Nezhukumatathil.
p. xi, Tomás Rivera - Dean Tomas Rivera, Gil Barrera Photographs of the University of Texas at San Antonio, MS 27, University of Texas Special Collections.
p. xi, Dalia Rosenfeld - Used by permission of Dalia Rosenfeld
p. 0, ©istock.com/lorenzoviolone
p. 3, AFP/AFP/Getty Images
p. 5, 20th Century Fox/Moviepix/Getty Images
p. 6, Matt Cardy/Getty Images News/Getty Images
p. 8, iStock.com/
p. 9, Peeter Viisimaa/iStock.com
p. 13, ©istock.com/ortlemma
p. 25, ©istock.com/ortlemma
p. 26, iStock.com/ValentinaPhotos
p. 27, iStock.com/ValentinaPhotos
p. 28, iStock.com/yipengge
p. 29, iStock.com/yipengge
p. 30, ©istock.com/ortlemma
p. 31, ©iStock.com/PeopleImages
p. 34, ©iStock.com/SonerCdem
p. 35, Boston Globe/Boston Globe/Getty Images
p. 38, Public Domain Image
p. 39, Fotosearch/Archive Photos/Getty Images
p. 41, Public Domain Image
p. 42, iStock.com/ThomasVogel
p. 43, iStock.com/ThomasVogel
p. 44, iStock.com/DNY59
p. 45, iStock.com/DNY59
p. 48, Public Domain Image
p. 49, ©iStock.com/Michael Warren
p. 59, ©iStock.com/Michael Warren
p. 60, iStock.com/ThomasVogel
p. 61, iStock.com/ThomasVogel
p. 62, iStock.com/pixhook

p. 63, iStock.com/pixhook
p. 64, iStock.com/
p. 65, iStock.com/
p. 66, ©iStock.com/Michael Warren
p. 67, iStock.com/borchee
p. 73, iStock.com/borchee
p. 74, iStock.com/LdF
p. 75, iStock.com/LdF
p. 76, iStock.com/borchee
p. 77, iStock.com/mustafagull
p. 81, ©istock.com/Coquinho
p. 87, ©istock.com/_creativedot_
p. 90, iStock.com/221A
p. 91, Picturenow/Universal Images Group/Getty Images
p. 92, iStock.com/221A
p. 92iStock.com/221A
p. 93, iStock.com/Andrey_A
p. 94, iStock.com/Andrey_A
p. 95, iStock.com/221A
p. 96, ©istock.com/LeoPatrizi
p. 100, iStock.com/hanibaram, iStock.com/seb_ra, iStock.com/Martin Barraud
p. 101, iStock.com/Martin Barraud
p. 103, StudySync
p. 103, StudySync
p. 104, StudySync
p. 105, StudySync
p. 106, StudySync
p. 107, James D. Morgan/Getty Images News/Getty Images
p. 108, StudySync
p. 108, StudySync
p. 109, NBC Universal Archives
p. 110, StudySync
p. 114, iStock.com/BilevichOlga
p. 117, iStock.com/Mutlu Kurtbas
p. 120, iStock.com/Martin Barraud
p. 123, iStock.com/DNY59
p. 125, iStock.com/Martin Barraud
p. 133, iStock.com/Jeff_Hu
p. 135, iStock.com/peepo
p. 138, iStock.com/tofumax
p. 142, iStock.com/polesnoy
p. 145, iStock.com/SasinParaksa
p. 148, iStock.com/Martin Barraud
p. 151, iStock.com/
p. 153, iStock.com/
p. 155, iStock.com/
p. 157, iStock.com/Martin Barraud
p. 159, iStock.com/Stígur Már Karlsson/Heimsmyndir
p. 160, iStock.com/
p. 160, iStock.com/
p. 160, iStock.com/
p. 160, iStock.com/
p. 160, iStock.com/
p. 164, iStock.com/Stígur Már Karlsson/Heimsmyndir
p. 165, iStock.com/Ales_Utovko
p. 167, iStock.com/kyoshino
p. 169, iStock.com/Stígur Már Karlsson/Heimsmyndir
p. 170, Universal History Archive/Getty Images
p. 171, iStock.com
p. 171, iStock.com
p. 171, iStock.com
p. 171, iStock.com
p. 171, iStock.com
p. 173, Universal History Archive/Getty Images
p. 174, iStock.com/BlackJack3D
p. 176, iStock.com/RazvanDP
p. 179, Universal History Archive/Getty Images

studysync

Text Fulfillment Through StudySync

If you are interested in specific titles, please fill out the form below and we will check availability through our partners.

ORDER DETAILS

Date:

TITLE	AUTHOR	Paperback/ Hardcover	Specific Edition *If Applicable*	Quantity

SHIPPING INFORMATION

Contact:

Title:

School/District:

Address Line 1:

Address Line 2:

Zip or Postal Code:

Phone:

Mobile:

Email:

BILLING INFORMATION ☐ SAME AS SHIPPING

Contact:

Title:

School/District:

Address Line 1:

Address Line 2:

Zip or Postal Code:

Phone:

Mobile:

Email:

PAYMENT INFORMATION

☐ CREDIT CARD

Name on Card:

Card Number:

Expiration Date:

Security Code:

☐ PO

Purchase Order Number:

StudySync Text Fulfillment, BookheadEd Learning, LLC
610 Daniel Young Drive | Sonoma, CA 95476